IN THE STEPS OF
BURKE & WILLS

IN THE STEPS OF BURKE & WILLS

TOM BERGIN

Published by the Australian Broadcasting Commission
145-153 Elizabeth Street, Sydney, NSW
Postal Address: GPO Box 487, Sydney 2001

Printed in Australia by Griffin Press Limited
© Australian Broadcasting Commission 1981

National Library of Australia card number
and ISBN 0 642 974136

Typesetting by Dalley Photocomposition
Text type: Aster 10 on 12

Designed by Tony Denny

Edited by Nina Riemer and Helen Findlay

Maps by Ewart Collings

Etchings supplied by the National Library, Canberra

Stills supplied by Kathie Atkinson, Mount Isa Mines,
Joseph J Scherschel © National Geographic Society
and the author

Photographs of paintings supplied by
La Trobe collection, State Library of Victoria

This book is dedicated to
the courageous men who died on the original
expedition, 1860-61

Charles Grey	died 17 April 1861	Lake Massacre
Charles Stone	died 22 April 1861	Bulloo Swamps
William Purcell	died 23 April 1861	Bulloo Swamps
Ludwig Becker	died 29 April 1861	Bulloo Swamps
William Patton	died 6 June 1861	Mud Plain
William Wills	died *c* 28 June 1861	Cooper's Creek
Robert Burke	died *c* 29 June 1861	Cooper's Creek

But is especially dedicated
to our brother and comrade
Greg McHugh
who died with equal bravery
5 June 1977

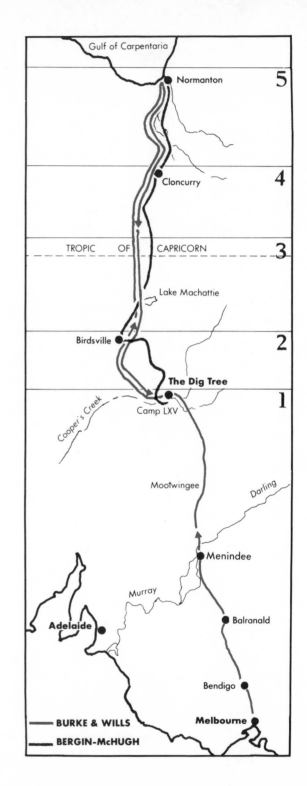

Gulf of Carpentaria

Normanton

5

Cloncurry

4

TROPIC OF CAPRICORN

3

Lake Machattie

Birdsville

2

The Dig Tree

Camp LXV

1

Cooper's Creek

Mootwingee

Darling

Menindee

Murray

Adelaide

Balranald

Bendigo

Melbourne

━━━ **BURKE & WILLS**
━━━ **BERGIN-McHUGH**

Darwin

AUSTRALIA

Perth

Brisbane

Adelaide
Melbourne

Sydney

Hobart

CONTENTS

PREFACE

Tom Bergin's association with the history department at the University of New England began with an extraordinary coincidence. On Sunday night, February 6, 1977, I watched the BBC television film on the Burke and Wills expedition; the following day I received a letter from Tom, then curator of mammals at Taronga Zoo, suggesting that he might enrol as a candidate for a Master's Degree in history, to study the causes of the expedition's failure. Professor Russel Ward was immediately interested in Bergin's proposal, which was, in part, to test his belief that the disasters of 1861, including the deaths of the two leaders, resulted substantially from related errors in the timing of the journey and the use of camels.

As the author explains, he had formed the view that Burke's greatest mistake in planning the dash on camels from Cooper's Creek to the Gulf and back, lay in the decision to depart at the height of summer. Men and beasts were thus subjected first to the intense heat of desert regions, then to the 'stupefying humidity' of the northern tropical monsoon. Camels, he argued, were wildly inappropriate as vehicles; with their 'soup plate' feet immersed in the mud of the wet season, the beasts would be virtually immobilised. Far better, Bergin thought, to travel in the dry northern winter. He estimated that Burke could have made it safely to the Gulf and back to Cooper's Creek, using camels, in the three months provided for with food stores, if he had travelled in a favourable season of the year. His journey in the winter of 1977 was an attempt to demonstrate the correctness of this estimate.

Although Tom Bergin's expedition failed in its principal object, it afforded experiences which will vastly enhance his ability to interpret and judge the journey of Burke and Wills. It is an adage of historians that the practitioner should be equipped with a stout pair of boots. But to attempt a 1600-mile journey by camel! This is surely an excess of zeal, and I am bound to say that this history department is not usually so rigorous in its fieldwork requirements. As Tom pointed out rather acidly, in reply to my request for evidence of his having studied history at a tertiary level:

I suggest that anyone persevering in a year's frustrating amateur fact finding, and prepared to cross, by camel, 1600 miles of some of the worst country of Australia, is displaying more than a passing interest in this particular aspect of history.

For the exploration buff, the great value of Bergin's painful journey in the tracks of Burke and Wills is to reveal the inaccuracy of the surviving maps. As the author realised from his own experience, Wills, though an astronomer, was unable in the circumstances of a forced march to ascertain longitude by star sightings, and therefore was dependent on compass readings, which have an error in that region of about six degrees. Thus the party arrived at the Flinders River, instead of the Albert, a good way to the west. Tom learned also, in the best school in the world, why it was that Burke made such little use of local game, and thus subjected his people to fatal deficiency diseases. When your timetable imposes on you a darg of twenty miles a day, it is a big consideration to halt progress in order to hunt. Camels are less flexible than horses, and cannot readily be detached from a train in search of game.

But the wider significance of this book, and its appeal for the general reader, rest on its sparkling literary qualities, and the fascination of the story it recounts. Tom Bergin has the observant eye of the scientist, and this is important in shaping his perception of the region, and explaining the disaster of Burke and Wills. He possesses also the artist's eye for detail and a natural flair with words; we have in consequence a rattling good yarn. I'm sure the profession of history will be grateful for the adventurous step across the disciplines of zoology and history which Tom invited us to share with him in 1977.

A T Yarwood
Associate Professor in History
University of New England

PROLOGUE

It is typical of Australia as a nation that we have no monument of any great national significance: no Liberty Bell, no Nelson's Column, no Arc de Triomphe, no symbols of victory. Instead our national attitudes towards human endeavour are best symbolised by two trees that stand as reminders, not only of heroism but also of cruel and inevitable defeat. One tree is 'Lone Pine' which stood on a ridge high over Gallipoli, a beach in the Dardanelles where the loss of thousands of Australian lives helped shape our identity and self-image as Anzacs. The other is the 'Dig Tree' in Central Australia, a giant coolibah tree which cast its shade over an earlier scene of heroic, hopeless defeat. For it was there, on April 21, 1861, that the two explorers, Burke and Wills, returned from crossing the Australian continent only to find that those on whom they depended for their lives had left that very day. Despite the store of provisions buried beneath the 'Dig' message blazed on the tree, they were doomed to a slow and lingering death on this lonely creek.

The 'Dig Tree' stands on a high knoll on the banks of Cooper's Creek, shading the southern end of a magnificent waterhole. The banks are steep and covered in thick green lignum bush, above which countless thousands of green grass parrots, corellas and galahs fight for perches in the tall coolibah trees and river red gums. The waterhole is teeming with fish, providing a haven for the pelicans, herons and cormorants which abound on the creek. As Burke and Wills trekked back from the Gulf their memory of this enchanting spot must have grown more vivid with each agonising step, until it seemed like paradise. So much greater a shock would it have been, then, to find themselves abandoned and dying here. When I stood, as they had, beneath the 'Dig Tree', it was hard to imagine death in the midst of all that life, unless the men who frantically scraped the earth beneath the 'Dig Tree' had already pushed themselves beyond a point of no return; doomed souls acting out a painful last scenario until they finally dropped.

It is a fact that tragedy is the greater when the means of avoiding it is near. Had destiny altered the course of any one of a dozen events for Burke and Wills they would have returned home victorious to claim the glory Burke so dearly sought. Had the depot party remained but nine more hours, had the relief party arrived one week earlier or dug up Burke's despatch beneath the 'Dig Tree', had they noticed Burke's tracks, had Burke rested three weeks beneath the 'Dig Tree', any one of these could have altered the course of history. But the fact is that fate did not alter a single dice-throw in Burke's favour, and we are left with the 'Dig Tree' to remind us of their suffering, their heroism and their deaths.

Many people since then have felt that their heroic deaths cannot simply be attributed to the hand of fate, and the blame for failure has legally and historically been placed at the feet of Burke and some of his officers. Surely, however, one cannot apportion blame until all the facts are available, and, more than that, one must understand the facts to interpret their significance.

Thus, to understand the mystery of the 'Dig Tree' one must become familiar with the country which delayed Burke, with the animals on which he depended, the food the party ate and the life led on such an expedition. It is only then that one can weigh up the bases of crucial decisions and perhaps understand what at first appear to be senseless moves.

In 1860 Burke set out North from the 'Dig Tree' with four men: himself a police officer; Wills, an astronomer; King, a soldier; and Grey, a rouseabout sailor. In 1977 we four stood beneath the same tree; myself, a scientist; Paddy, a cameleer; Nugget, an elder of the Pitjantjatjara; and Frankie, an Arunda youth, Nugget's son. It was to unravel the mystery of the 'Dig Tree' that we stood there. We had come to retrace the steps of Burke and Wills.

THE FIRST STEP

'A journey of a thousand miles begins with one step.'
Lao Tse

It was a bleak wintry day when they buried my friend, Greg, whom destiny had denied the chance to see our dreams become reality. Our expedition had been as dogged by setbacks as was the original expedition; initially by the sudden withdrawal of financial backing, then by massive floods out west and, finally, by a fatal disease, leukaemia, which dashed Greg's hopes of following the trail blazed by Burke and Wills.

Greg was never the type to let anything upset him; he simply arranged for his brother, Paddy, to take his place, and continued to share his part in setting up the expedition from his hospital bed. We were not to let his death delay or prevent the trip, he kept insisting, go while the season lasts. Paddy I had met only a few times and, although he lacked Greg's experience, he had handled camels before. In fact, like many bushmen you meet, he had done quite a number of things before: plumbing, welding, parachuting and fencing. At present he was breaking in a few of the camels which Greg had selected for the trip.

One of the biggest problems to overcome was locating the other two who were to accompany us, Nugget Gnalkenga and Frankie. Nugget was an old friend of Greg's who had ridden with him on his long trek and so had experienced the type of journey we were about to undertake. He was an elder of the Pitjantjatjara people, and he and his son Frankie were supposed to have been seen at the Hermannsberg Mission in Central Australia, but we had had great difficulty trying to reach them. When we finally did contact them, and they agreed to come, we were delighted. It would make a team of four, the same as Burke's original team on the final dash to the Gulf.

The Victorian Exploring Expedition had set out from Melbourne on August 19, 1860, with great fanfare; eighteen men strong with twenty-seven camels, twenty-three horses and seven heavily loaded drays.* It was the most lavishly equipped expedition in Australian history, and at its head rode Robert O'Hara Burke, whose choice as leader had aroused some comment in the colony. Second in charge was George Landells, a self-styled 'camel expert'. The expedition also included William Wills, a surveyor; Herman Beckler, a doctor; and Ludwig Becker, an artist; as well as a foreman, nine general hands and three Pathan camel drivers. The expedition had been organised by a committee of the Royal Society of Victoria and was financed by a grant of six thousand pounds from the government and three thousand pounds from public subscriptions. Its purpose: to explore the country between Cooper's Creek in central Australia, and the Gulf of Carpentaria. Nearly twenty years earlier Captain Charles Sturt had surveyed the Cooper's Creek region, while at the same time (1844-45) Ludwig Leichhardt had explored the country far to the north around the Gulf of Carpentaria. Between their paths lay a vast tract of unexplored land. If a trade route could be found from Melbourne to Cooper's Creek, and from there to the Gulf, it was thought that Victoria's influence would be greatly increased. But Victoria was not the only colony to see the potential of links with the north. The South Australian Government had offered a reward of two thousand pounds to the first man to cross the continent from south to north. Five months earlier an expedition, led by John McDouall Stuart, had set out from Adelaide. It was to be a race, and Burke, the dashing Irish cavalry officer, was determined to overtake the cautious Scot. But within five weeks Burke had realised that his unwieldly entourage, with four-ton wagons, was unlikely to overtake the South Australian expedition or anyone else. Like many other explorers he discovered that drays and wagons are cumbersome, awkward things once off hard roads, and his were loaded to the axles. At a couple of places along the way he had auctioned or sold off stores, notable amongst them eight casks of lime juice which had been taken to prevent scurvy. Although Dr Beckler was in charge of stores it seems that Burke often interfered. Burke was obviously a difficult man and by the time the expedition reached Menindee, the outpost of civilisation, four hundred and fifty miles north of Melbourne on the Darling River, serious rifts had occurred within the party. Half of the original eighteen men had resigned or been sacked, most notably Landells, the second-in-command, and Dr Beckler.

Landells seems to have been a troublemaker and he and Burke clashed head-on several times. He also seems to have been either reasonably ignorant of camels or a bloody liar, having insisted on bringing sixty gallons of rum along to stop 'camel scurvy', a cure which a number of men availed themselves of, leading to Landells' dismissal. This left a gap as only the two sepoys, Belooch and Dost Mahommed, knew anything

---

* For a vivid and accurate description of the events surrounding the expedition and the factors leading up to it the reader is referred to *Cooper's Creek* by Alan Moorehead, published by Hamish Hamilton, London, 1963.

The Great Australian Exploration Race

about camels, and only King, who had served in the army in India, spoke their language. He was put in charge of camels and promptly allowed the sepoys to hobble them, a sensible and time-saving procedure which Landells disdained. William Wills, the quiet young Devonshire surveyor, was promoted to second-in-command, and Burke put on new men, including 'Charlie' Grey, a sailor-turned-bushman he met on the way.

At Menindee he had to spell the stock and during his three-week rest reconsider his whole mode of progress. Ahead the country was largely unknown and on the experience of the last five weeks there was no guarantee at all that drays would get through. If he loaded the stores and equipment onto the horses and camels he would be able to travel much faster. But with all his camels fully loaded at four hundred pounds each, and his horses at around one hundred and twenty pounds, he could still only carry five tons-odd, a quarter of the remaining stores. And he had nowhere near enough packsaddles for forty-nine-odd horses and camels, so his carrying capacity was reduced to about half of that. The locals, who had some knowledge of the country to the north, warned him that the few waterholes out there were drying up fast. Burke could either make a dash for Cooper's Creek with provisions for six months or so, or wait several months at Menindee until the next good season and re-organise his team meanwhile. But if he waited until the next good rains, Stuart would win, and the citizens of Victoria would be most unimpressed to hear that their widely publicised expedition had been halted only two weeks' ride north of Melbourne. He decided to go, leaving a depot of stores at Menindee to be brought up later. Several of his stock were not fit to travel, and these he would have to leave behind, as well as those without saddles. He also cut his men back, leaving Dr Beckler (who had already resigned, but who agreed to stay on and look after the depot), Ludwig Becker, too old to be of use and only an artist anyway, and a Pathan to look after the camels. He also left behind Hodgkinson, a young reporter who had been following the expedition, and a couple of hands he had taken on as replacements. On October 19, 1860, he left Menindee for Cooper's Creek with eight men, fifteen horses, sixteen camels and six months' supply of stores. Had he returned within six months his decision to leave part of his party here would have been seen as magnificent foresight. Instead, since he did not return, it was condemned as rash and erroneous, although no one as yet has suggested what the right course of action might have been. It is laughable to imagine Burke's critics chasing off across the country which now lay ahead of him, a stretch of land which had nearly claimed the life of Sturt fifteen years earlier. Burke was, if nothing else, a very brave man. By chance, he had encountered a man who knew this country, one William Wright, who agreed to guide them as far as the Torowatto Swamps far to the north. Guide them he did; they made it safely across two hundred miles of endless plain in ten days.

During the time Wright spent with the expedition, Burke must have been impressed by the man and his bushmanship for he offered him the position of third officer of the expedition provided that the committee back in Melbourne had not already appointed someone to replace Landells. Burke has been critised for this on the grounds 'that he knew so little about Wright'. I can only say that after a man has led you through two hundred miles of bush, you have a good idea of his bushmanship or lack of it.

In any event Wright accepted the offer and, having arranged for Aboriginal guides to take the expedition on to Cooper's Creek, he and his two.trackers returned to Menindee. His task: to assemble a relief team and bring the remainder of the stores up to Cooper's Creek.

How was he to do it? He had at his disposal an old German artist, a young reporter, a sepoy and a saddler. Not many, when you consider the task at hand—to take up to fifteen-odd tons of stores to Cooper's Creek. In addition he had only seven horses and nine camels, and these were 'inferior in carrying powers', since Burke had taken the fittest animals.

However, Burke had told him that he would probably send back a team of pack animals to help convey the stores up. This was a crucial mistake; there is no room for 'probably' or 'maybe' in that country. Wright later

Robert O'Hara Burke

remarked that 'in fact, Mr. Burke used to alter his mind so very often at different times, it was not possible to understand what he really did mean'. A few days after Wright returned to Menindee, Burke struck Cooper's Creek and, following some incidents with the Aboriginals there, he decided he could not spare any of the men to take the pack-team back. In fact, after a while he seems to have forgotten all about the arrangement, and referred to Wright's 'being up in a few days'.

Even in 1977, more than one hundred years later, it still took us 'a few days' to get our equipment organised and get it to Cooper's Creek.

Not long after Greg's funeral I loaded all the food, medical supplies and radio and navigation equipment onto a four-wheel-drive and, with a sad farewell to the family, set out for Dubbo where I was to meet up with the rest of the team. My driver was an old friend, Dave Cody, the head mammal keeper at Taronga Zoo, who was shortly to embark on an even stranger venture: he was to fly to England and bring back four African elephants, one, a bull, as deck freight on a cargo ship. Thus, we should have had plenty to talk about, but the prospects of the task ahead, the enormity of which had, I think, only just hit me, left me with a lot to think about and little to say.

Paddy and the camels were already there when we arrived, and Nugget and Frankie came up soon afterwards, having flown across from Alice Springs. When our bedrolls and provisions were heaped up alongside the saddles and saddlebags, watertanks and harness, which Paddy had arranged, the pile looked awesome. We were soon hard at it, packing everything into the saddlebags and giving the camels some last-minute treatment. With that over, we had some last-minute treatment ourselves from our doctor, who kindly drove up to give us all our final check-ups and tetanus boosters.

When at last everything seemed in order, checked and double-checked, we fed the camels, unrolled our swags around the fire and, in the frosty winter's night, did our best to get some sleep. When dawn came and we roused ourselves, the outline of heads and hands was clearly marked on our pillows by dark areas where no frost had fallen. I remember how we told ourselves, as we rubbed frozen hands in front of the fire, that this was one problem we wouldn't face in the desert. We were dead wrong.

The camels, desert-bred and chosen not for their table manners but for stamina, refused to be loaded into the waiting truck, and it was all we could do with the help of the truck drivers to tow them in inch by struggling inch. Once inside, each camel was 'hushed down' into a kneeling position, a position they can maintain for days quite comfortably in a desert sandstorm, being equipped with horny pads on knees and chest to take the weight. The way they go down is one of the most awkward movements I have ever seen, and it is an even more awkward sensation when you are actually riding the beast.

On the order 'hush' the camel stops still and roars continuously while he looks around at the terrain. Camels are reluctant to hush down on stony or sloping ground. Having selected a spot, the animal first drops forward onto its knees, flinging the rider forward, then rocks abruptly back onto its haunches, flicking the inexperienced rider back through a ninety-degree arc. Just when it seems that the rider is destined to dismount backwards over the rump, the camel lowers the forelegs and comes to rest on its elbows, after which the rider rocks forward, slightly dazed, to assume his original vertical position. In rising, the whole process is carried out in reverse order, and is even more abrupt.

Camels do not have a natural instinct to rise or kneel on command, so Greg and Paddy had spent many bruising hours in the stockyards trying to replace the natural tendencies of biting and kicking with these virtues. They all seemed to have forgotten them on our first day, considerably delaying our departure from Dubbo. Luckily the three hundred and fifty miles to the town of Wilcannia was all straight, sealed highway, and our truck and Land-Rover, towing a trailer, managed it with only one breakdown on the way. Wilcannia is a former paddle-steamer port on the Darling River, about eighty miles upstream from Burke's depot at Menindee. The night was bitterly cold and the moon well up when we reached town, and we unloaded the camels by the light of the headlights, a process we had been dreading but which went without a hitch. We rolled out our swags around the fire, and fortified ourselves against the cold wind with meat pies and rum before turning in. The fire blew out sometime during the night and the thermometer showed two degrees below zero at first light, but the thick ice on the water troughs indicated that the temperature may have been lower still.

Loading the camels proved just as difficult as it had been at Dubbo, and we paused in town to make last minute 'phone calls and buy the few bits and pieces which are always overlooked. We were soon heading northwards on a narrow dirt track parallel to Burke's route, arriving in the tiny opal-mining settlement of White Cliffs at midday. We paused to ask directions but no one seemed to know which was the track to Tibooburra, so we took a consensus of opinion and headed off. Road maps in this part of the world are worse than useless; they are dangerously misleading and, where ours showed a nice straight graded road, we found ourselves on a rough bush track which wound across bull dust flats and up over endless dunes unless it finally dissipated into a fan of old divergent tyre tracks.

Dusk fell as we topped the red dunes which form the southern shore of the Bulloo overflow. Normally a dry mud plain, for the last few years it has been full, forming an inland sea which has completely cut off Tibooburra from the east, unless one goes over the dunes. We ground our way around it in the dark, hour after hour, driving completely by instinct, picking up car tracks for a while and then losing them again.

Just as it seemed we were destined to camp there the night, the headlights picked up the signpost on the western edge of the overflow telling motorists to turn back. We bumped down onto the dusty road and,

William John Wills

tired and hungry, followed it the fifty or so miles into Tibooburra.

This is one of the most pleasant little settlements in the outback, its position on the edge-of-beyond lends it a frontier atmosphere where everyone must help everyone else. In Sydney I have seen hundreds of cars drive on past a woman whose car had broken down in pouring rain, but up near Tibooburra, if you pull up to stretch your legs the first car will stop and make sure nothing is wrong. True to form, everyone in the old Family Hotel turned out to help us unload the camels who behaved perfectly this time, and gave us enough time for a cold beer before bed. Most of us, I think, dreamt all night of interminable dunes and mulga scrub, rising and falling in the light of the headlights.

The wide main street and the row of old stone houses appeared in the light of dawn like an apparition from the last century, even down to the solitary donkey wandering across the street in a cloud of flies. Tibooburra has two hotels and local tradition dictates that after a few drinks in one, you wander over and have a few in the other, so we followed the donkey and tradition across to the other hotel, The Tibooburra, for breakfast.

Fortified, and with our spare petrol drums full, we set out north across the rolling treeless downs to the Queensland border. An hour or so beyond the border the countryside changed, and the track wound through myall scrub until a few miles from Orientos homestead, when the first dunes and deep channel crossings appeared. These latter consist of soft wet sand, and we hit the first one unprepared and found ourselves bogged to the axles. The next hour or so was spent digging the Land Rover out of the bog and cutting scrub to lay under the tyres.

We stood hot and sweaty on the far bank for another hour waiting for the camel truck which had been following some hours behind us, and had had to pull up and refuel from the spare fuel drum a couple of times. We managed to winch it across without too much trouble and headed west again, to arrive at the ice cold waters of Cooper's Creek long after nightfall. It was a weary team which lay down to rest that night, but at least we had decided to have a day's rest here while the equipment was finally assembled, so we slept soundly.

The one day's preparation here soon became two days, what with the packing and repacking and the shedding of all those things which, although they may come in handy, are not absolutely essential. Even some of the food had to be abandoned.

At last, after a year's preparation and numerous setbacks, we were ready to set out in the tracks of Burke and Wills.

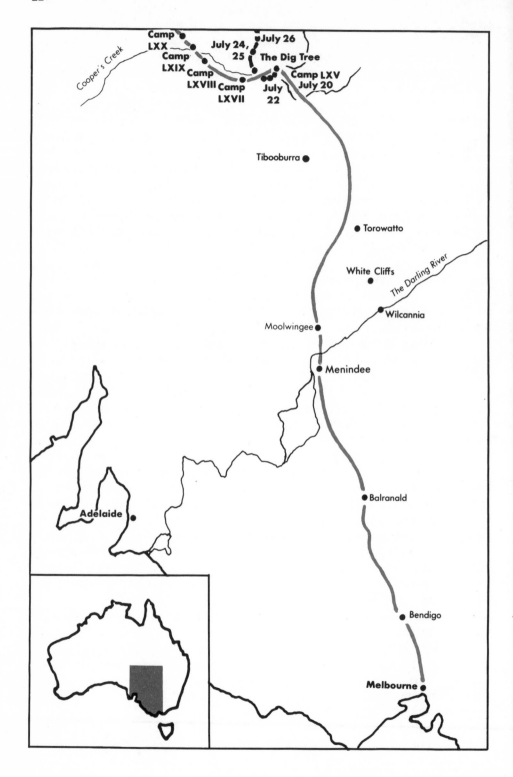

Camp LXX

July 24, 25

July 26

The Dig Tree

Camp LXIX

Camp LXVIII

Camp LXVII

July 22

Camp LXV
July 20

Cooper's Creek

Tibooburra

Torowatto

White Cliffs

The Darling River

Wilcannia

Moolwingee

Menindee

Adelaide

Balranald

Bendigo

Melbourne

THE LAND OF STONE

We left the 'Dig Tree' camp on July 22, a fine cool morning, two days late. The 'Dig Tree' still stands today, a gnarled old coolibah scarred with the blaze and the fatal inscription, although the bark has grown over most of the letters now. It was easy to see why Burke had chosen that spot as a camp site, high on the bank of the big Bullo Bullo waterhole, shaded by coolibahs and with good grazing on the verbena flats nearby. The waterhole was full of yellowbelly which attracted the numerous pelicans, cormorants and other waterfowl. The truck drivers and a small group of onlookers gave us a rousing farewell and I suppose it should have been an exciting moment, but, frankly, I was so worried about the bacon and biltong—dried and salted meat—we had been forced to leave behind that I felt no elation.

The river was running fast and was two feet deep over the crossing. It was ice cold. The camels must have sensed our apprehension for they broke file as we approached the river, and formed a tangle of ropes, camels and baggage, kicking and bucking all over the place. We managed to sort them out after much cursing, and led them towards the river on foot, which they forded without a moment's hesitation, much to my relief, as I had it on good authority that camels are reluctant to cross water. We paused to fill the tanks, then set off. Our route lay due west, parallel to Cooper's Creek.

After half a mile the lush verbena and Coolibah flats gave way to a high stony plateau, devoid of life but for dead grass and the odd bit of salt-bush. Away to the south the plateau petered out into the sand dunes and to the north-east stood a range of barren peaks. The going was slow and marred by the camels continually breaking pace, causing saddle straps, baggage clips and tempers to give way frequently. Blisters started to appear on heels and bottoms.

We made camp that night in a solitary group of stunted gum on a vast claypan, only fourteen miles from the 'Dig Tree'. After a supper of bacon and rolled oats I lay awake stiff and sore, wondering what the family was doing at home, or, for that matter, what the hell I was doing here. What had possessed me to give up a good job in the city and come all this way out here, only to find myself lying on a claypan in the icy wind of the desert night?

As I lay shivering I tried to pinpoint the moment when my casual interest in the fate of the two explorers became a determination to set the record straight. I think it happened gradually, minor irritation slowly turning to anger as I read one armchair critic after another pontificating on the mistakes of the expedition. The Commission of Enquiry in 1861, for example, could not understand why the relief expedition, once it had bought horses, did not simply throw all the supplies on them and take off next day, never mind the lack of packsaddles or the fact that the horses were yet to be broken in. Such trivia did not interest the Commissioners, worthy politicians, who were to cast judgment upon Burke and his officers without the slightest idea of camels or deserts, of hunger or scurvy. In fact, they wouldn't have known which end of a camel they were looking at.

It almost seemed as if the facts were irrelevant as long as they had a scapegoat to give to the colony's angry public. And writers ever since had done little more than echo their findings, branding Burke as a fool, Brahé a deserter and Wright a dithering incompetent. No one had asked the two basic questions: why did the camels die and why did the men die? Were the camels overloaded? Did they go too fast? Did they die of some disease, or what? It is simply not enough to say, as the historian Manning Clark did, that Burke suffered from attacks of the sillies. One must actually show how an error of judgment on Burke's part led to the disaster. Was he mad to think he could get to the Gulf and back to Cooper's Creek in twelve weeks? Had Burke not been trapped in the mud up north could he have made it back in time and returned a conquering hero? I was convinced that the major cause of Burke's disaster was in the timing of his trip to the Gulf. He left Cooper's Creek in the height of summer, subjecting his men and beasts to the intense heat of the central deserts and then to the mud, rain and stupefying humidity of the monsoon season in the tropical North.

Camels have feet like soup plates, perfect for walking on sand but almost impossible to pull out of mud. Once the 'soup plate' is covered with a foot or two of mud, the camel is virtually immobilised. How could anyone in their right mind take camels into the tropics in the wet season? After all, the seasonal conditions of the North had been well known for many years in Burke's day. Burke seemed not to have considered the camels' susceptibility to wet conditions, but to have been blinded by their ability to survive without water. Earlier explorers with horses, and often sheep and cattle, had to rely on finding water as they went along. They used scouts, either Aboriginals or experienced white bushmen, to go ahead of the main party and map out a route from waterhole to waterhole. These scouts would then, while waiting for the main party to catch

up at the waterhole, pass the time by fishing or hunting, thus supplement-
ing the dried provisions.

But Burke had no need of this slow and cautious progress, for he had
camels. Independent of waterholes, he could set out on a compass bearing with no need of Aboriginal guides to find water for him, or to catch
the odd fish.

Here, too, he erred badly, for men and horses needed water, and the
camels would have to carry it. His water supply—for four men and their
horses—weighed 600 pounds, which meant heavy loads all round, less
food for each man, and no riding for anyone. I felt that had Burke used
Aboriginal guides, as for example Eyre and Leichhardt had done before
him, he would have had no need to carry that weight of water, and would
have found more useful food plants and animals into the bargain. Had
he done this in winter, I reasoned, he would have made the Gulf and back
on three months' provisions.

But all this was, of course, just a theory like all the others, and, one
hundred and twenty years after the original expedition, it was likely to
remain so. I used to sit and ruminate on it all in odd quiet moments, just
one more armchair expert developing his own biased theories.

It was then that I met Greg McHugh. He strode into my office one day,
a total stranger, sat himself down and without further ado asked: 'Do you
know anyone who wants to buy camels?' My visitor was tall and rangy
with a dark mane beneath his battered hat and a beard brushing his chest.
His skin was burned to leather and ingrained with the red dust of the
deserts, but his daunting appearance was offset by twinkling eyes and
a wide friendly grin. He was a camel trader from out west, down in the
'big smoke' for the camel races at the Royal Easter Show. As it happened
I was looking for some good breeding camels at the time, and so a deal
was quickly struck. As we yarned about camels and prices I raised the
question of Burke's dash to the Gulf. 'You know,' he said, 'it's funny you
should mention that because it has always fascinated me.'

That night after dinner we started sifting through the evidence, assess-
ing each decision in the light of Greg's experience. He had made many
long trips by camel, horse and donkey, and had a pretty good idea of just
how hard each type of beast can be pushed. His comments tended to confirm my thoughts. Pack camels can carry over two hundred pounds. They
can, if pushed, cover more than thirty miles a day and Greg had used
them on treks of sixteen hundred miles. Thus Burke's dash was not quite
so foolhardy as the critics supposed, and provided the camels did not
strike mud it was feasible to try to go from Cooper's Creek to the Gulf
and back in the twelve weeks he allowed. 'In fact' Greg said off-handedly,
'if a bloke did it in winter, it shouldn't be all that bad a trip.'

We looked up from the book-strewn desk and stared at each other for
a moment. A huge grin spread across his face. 'Why not?'

I thought for a minute. Apart from finding out exactly what problems
arise with camels on such a trip, it would be a great opportunity to see

the country first hand, and would certainly be the best way to test our theory. 'Why not?' I replied.

'Why not indeed?' I asked myself now as I lay on a claypan stiff and sore, with sixteen hundred miles ahead of me. Pulling my bluey closer around me I shivered and thought of my warm bed at home, and dozed fitfully, telling myself that I had found one good reason already.

The following day we broke camp at 8.30 am, and crossed our first sand dunes shortly afterwards. The camels handled the dunes well, but I became slightly anxious when I saw the deadly crotalaria or 'Desert Poison Bush' growing among these dunes. I need not have worried, for we later found that the camels would not touch it.

That day we settled into a steady pace and for the first time I realised what a camel team can do when they get into their rhythm. Walking alongside the team I was taking three paces to their one. The dunes soon gave way to gibber downs again, interspersed with stony bluffs. Cooper's Creek lay over to our right, a long green oasis in the barren plains.

Towards midday a cold wind sprang up from the south and was to stay with us all day, a similar blow having greeted Burke and Wills in this region:

18 Dec. 1861. A remarkable southerly squall came on between 5 and 6 pm, with every appearance of rain. The sky, however, soon cleared, but the wind continued to blow in a squally and irregular manner from the same quarter all evening.

A couple of times that morning I had noticed a strange shifting white mass up ahead. However, it always seemed to keep miles away, vanishing and reappearing at odd intervals. Shortly after lunch, as we topped yet another stony rise, we sighted one much closer in, a whirling mass of white and pink. By now we were so intrigued that we stopped and wasted a precious twenty minutes getting the binoculars out, but it was worth it. Through the glasses we could make out thousands and thousands of galahs and corellas shifting group by group across the plain, showing white or pink in flight, almost disappearing on the ground. What brought them there we never did discover, for the area, when we finally reached it, seemed just like the rest of the surrounding country. Perhaps the grass seeds or whatever it was had been completely cleaned up as the vast flocks moved on.

Overhead, solitary brown hawks circled endlessly, and we were unable to find out what they lived on either. A person would obviously need a long time in this barren country to come to grips with it and unearth its secrets.

The camels, fresh and now settled into their long swinging stride, made short work of the sixteen miles to Innaminka, and by 2.30 pm we were in sight of the ancient town. For a while last century it had been a thriving settlement with a hotel, hospital and police station, but was later abandoned. Today it stirs agains; its new demountable pub and Mike Steele's Trading Post stand amid old stone ruins and the heaps of broken bottles, but it boasts little else.

Our plan called for total abstinence, and complete self-reliance, to emulate the ordeal of Burke and Wills. But what the hell, I thought, we are going well, and a couple of beers before we face the desert will make little difference to our total calories over three months. So beer it was, and a bar of milk chocolate for Paddy, with some sweets for Frankie. Armed with these and two new waterbags we set out to camp on the other side of the Mulkonbar waterhole, only a few miles away. At this point the creek was barely four inches deep but all the curses we could muster would not get the camels across. They simply refused to go near the water, despite the fact that they'd happily walked through deeper water two days previously.

We tried each camel in turn, and each in turn refused in its characteristic way. Alice, firmly but gently, turned away; Ginger roared, bucked and spat all over me; while Larrikin nearly emasculated Paddy with a well-aimed strike. Wallaper stood stock still ignoring all efforts to budge him, his eyes fixed on Mecca or some other distant object. Paddymelon bolted back towards Innaminka,while Frances and Cleo got hopelessly tangled in a lignum bush. It was a fiasco, but twenty minutes later, hot and puffing, we had them back in order.

By now the sun had almost set and the water, which had shone like a mirror before, was now in shadow. The camels crossed it like lambs as if they had really been looking forward to it all day.

A blazing fire and a hot bowl of beef and biltong soup restored our spirits, and to show that *we* weren't scared of the water, we walked back through it for a last cold beer before facing the Stony Desert. It proved to be a wise precaution.

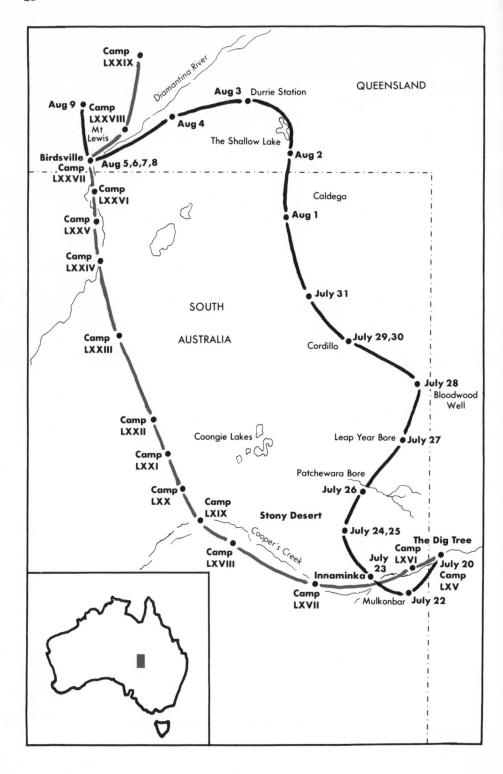

NORTH TO CORDILLO

Only a greater stillness in the air,
Save for hot sighs of desert-heated breath,
Only the stars, ceasing their sleepless stare,
Only the east, rose-flushing, fresh from death.
                                          Ernest Favenc

We woke with the first light of dawn and with a terrible sense of apprehension. Today we would hit Sturt's Stony Desert, this was *it*. I dragged myself out of the swag with that 'well, here goes' feeling I have experienced when running onto a grand final football field, or making the initial incision of a difficult operation, a mixture of excitement and dread.

I thought about a similar day for that earlier party and mused on their departure from Cooper's Creek. One of the faults in Burke's character, which so many were quick to point out, was his recklessness, and he has often been criticised for leaving Cooper's Creek as soon as he did. The Royal Commission of Enquiry in 1861 found that 'Mr. Burke evinced a far greater amount of zeal than prudence in finally departing from Cooper's Creek before the depot party had arrived from Menindee'.

Yet a quite reasonable explanation exists in a letter he wrote from Cooper's Creek just before they set out, a letter which was submitted to the court later on.

I did not intend to start so soon, but we have had some severe thunderstorms lately, with every appearance of a heavy fall of rain to the north, and as I have given the other route a fair trial, I do not wish to lose so favourable an opportunity.

The diary proves that in fact this was probably a good move, as he did strike water all through the desert. Burke's only knowledge of what lay ahead had come from Gregory's and Sturt's descriptions, and from Wills' recent adventures. All suggested that water would be vitally important in crossing this country.

We filled our water tanks to the brim in preparation for the arid country ahead. Burke had gone west from this point before turning north by west, thus avoiding much of the stone. We could not follow, for the floods had turned the Coongie Lakes into an inland sea. Instead, we were to head due north, on the route which Wills first attempted.

Of this northern route Burke remarks:

From Camp 63 we made frequent excursions in order to endeavour (in accordance with instructions) to find a practicable route northward, between Gregory and Sturt's track, but without success. Mr. Wills, upon one occasion, travelled ninety miles to the north without finding water, when his camels escaped, and he and the man who accompanied him were obliged to return on foot, which they accomplished in forty-eight hours ...

I am satisfied that a practicable route cannot be established in that direction, except during the rainy season or by sinking wells, as the natives have evidently lately abandoned that part of the country for want of water.

We were.only to appreciate Wills' worth when we saw that tract of land first-hand. Burke was obviously impressed enough by his report to choose a more westerly route for the main expedition.

It was 9.30 am before we got under way, every strap and buckle checked and nervously double checked. For the first mile or so all was grand, the track meandering through stunted eucalypt scrub on a plain of alluvial clay, but abruptly, as we topped a low rise, we found ourselves facing a sea of stone. Sturt had described the region thus: 'A stony desert covered with flints from one to six inches long which wore down the hooves of the horses almost to the quick'.

That day went badly. Ginger, leading on a halter, regarded the trip as a wandering smorgasbord, and turned aside to graze each tiny piece of saltbush or Parrakeelya he happened to pass. When this happened the other camels would pile up behind him in disarray, and Alice, thinking it was a scheduled stop, would promptly kneel, one or another of the others following suit.

About midday, just when the camels were again falling into a reasonable rhythm, there was a great crash from halfway down the line sending all the animals into a plunging frenzy. Wallaper and a watertank had parted company when a clip gave way, sending the full tank crashing onto the stone. As we dismounted to retrieve it we saw a large dark stain spreading over the red earth; our precious water was rapidly soaking away. Paddy repaired the hole as well as he could in the circumstances, stemming the flow to a trickle, and by tying the tank on with rawhide we were soon underway again.

On the western horizon ran a long sand dune while to the east stood a range of low, barren hills, blue and blurred by the heat haze. In between spread the vast plain of stone. Our progress was hard and slow, Ginger stopping at every saltbush in sight. Wallaper's load, one side lightened by a half-empty water tank, was considerably lopsided, and the tank on the other side hung so low it had severely chafed the poor beast's knee. Re-arrange the load as we might, we only succeeded in chafing his other knee. It was with bitter regret that we emptied out half of the water from the sound tank to even the load, cutting our capacity from thirty gallons to fifteen gallons.

We camped that night in a 'washaway', a dry gully carved out of the stone by flood erosion, defended when we arrived by a small brown wren whose call closely resembled a bellbird. Sore and weary, we dined on damper, curried peas and pork and copious soggy rice, a creation rarely mentioned by gourmets but a firm favourite in the desert.

Afterwards, having taken stock of the state of beasts, tanks and harness, we decided to stay the following day and repair our gear. From our camp we could see the ABC film crew, who followed us to shoot a documentary, camped further down the gully; two vehicles, a generator powering the arc lights which lit up tables, chairs, blow-up mattresses and iced beer, nostalgic reminders of the life we were leaving behind. Since we were, so to speak, their nearest neighbours, we dropped in and courteously shared a beer and a game of 'five hundred'. Back at our own camp, wrapped in balaclava and 'Bluey' coats against the freezing night winds, I took my star sightings before turning in. At dawn we were up treating saddle sores, patching and readjusting pack-saddles, testing our equipment. The venerable old Winchester rifle was shooting true, but the revolver jammed on a faulty round, and rather than take a chance on carrying it like that we buried it in the bank of the washaway. It was a sad moment as the revolver had been a gift from my father.

Over the billy the talk drifted from crook revolvers to crook camels, and to Ginger in particular. Camels are related to cattle in as much as they chew the cud, and thus camel bridles do not have a bit, which would interfere with their chewing. But the lack of a bit means that a straying or troublesome camel cannot be given the same 'gentle reminder' as a horse; thus they are often 'nose-pegged'. When this practice started is uncertain, but it has been used for thousands of years in the Middle East and the ritual procedures were taught to Nugget's father by an Afghan.

We decided that Ginger would have to be 'pegged', in order to stop his disrupting progress every second saltbush. Paddy went to get a nose-peg while Nugget rummaged through his swag and produced an evil-looking 'pegging stick'. I took one look at this device and offered to do the job myself using a nice sterile scalpel, disinfectant and a local anaesthetic. Nugget declined the offer, and said that knives had been tried years ago but caused too much bleeding. I had another close look at the pegging stick and saw his point. A scalpel is so sharp it cuts whatever it crosses, blood vessels included. The wooden stick, although quite pointed, is blunt by comparison and pierces skin but pushes large blood vessels aside. This principle is used extensively in modern surgery in what is termed 'blunt dissection'.

We decided to do it the 'proper Afghan way', but compromised between the old and the new by thoroughly disinfecting the pegging stick. Paddy returned with the small wooden nose-peg, the shape of the chess piece known as the 'bishop'. In fact they resemble each other so closely I am sure they have a common origin, and since the bishop always goes off on a tangent, as do camels, I am even more certain of the connection.

Over another billy (this being a rest day, we had several billies) Paddy and Nugget explained to me the reasons for the size and shape of the wooden peg. It must be strong enough so that a moderate tug on it does not break it, yet weak enough so that if the line attached to the peg is caught in a tree, or trodden on, the peg will snap rather than have the base pulled through the unfortunate beast's nose. Thus the size of the shaft must be neither too thick nor too thin but just so, and suitable types of wood have been determined over countless centuries, too soft or too hard having been eliminated, as also were those which gave off irritant resins. Metal is no good as it gets too hot, and plastics have been used but are too hard.

As the smoke drifted up I wondered how many ancient camp fires had been spent over this same discussion. It was a great effort to overcome lethargy and substitute action for discussion. Susan Chitty, a fascinating lady who crossed the European Alps on donkeys, remarked that it is more effort to move five yards on a rest day than to walk fifteen miles any other day. She was right, too.

Ginger was duly roped and tied tight, and the operation was over in a moment. It is certainly no more cruel than nose-rings in bulls or pigs, and less traumatic than docking horses' and dogs' tails, which procedures have little good reason to be done other than the whim of fashion. Ginger was, however, not impressed, and roared his distaste across the plain.

After a meagre lunch, a stick of biltong and piece of damper each, Paddy decided to go shooting. As this seemed to the rest of us to be a complete waste of time in these parts, he went alone. Nugget and Frankie curled up for a kip beside the fire, while I checked out the radio and took some sun sightings on the sextant.

We settled back to rest and were dozing fitfully, plagued by flies, when awoken by wild war whoops from a ridge to the north. Paddy had shot an emu, and Frankie raced out to help him drag it into camp. Amidst a cloud of flies the old man sliced off the prime meat, carefully scraping the fat off from the inside of the skin along the back. He heated the fat in the frypan to release the oil and the best cuts of meat were then fried in it; the rest was boiled up in the billies. I found the black meat delicious, a bit stringy but rich and gamey, a great change from biltong. The boiled meat is salted and eaten cold over the next few days. Although little was wasted I never quite brought myself to eat the most prized portion, the claws. With a full stomach of fried and boiled birdie, and a billy full for tomorrow, we slept soundly.

The next day we were rearing to go, not so the camels. Wallaper responded to my efforts to hush him with a lightning-fast kick to my

Above: The 'Dig Tree'

Overleaf: Paddy McHugh and Tom Bergin roping Cleo down at Dubbo

Following: Paddy McHugh saddles Paddymelon
The Bergin-McHugh expedition on the move

stomach, his standard response to most things. Ginger topped that by regurgitating a couple of gallons of digesta over Frankie and me. We hit the road late, and our progress was often interrupted by the film crew, so that by mid-morning we were quite relieved to see them depart. The feeling was mixed with other sensations, however, for now we were quite alone in the desert, and its silence and stillness seemed to close in and engulf us. We could have been the only living things on this earth, nothing else stirred from horizon to horizon. To the east the mountains were closer now, jagged, jumbled piles of bare rock, glinting occasionally in the sun like suburban rooftops.

The going was hard and the pace telling for the first time, but by now Ginger was concentrating on the walk and the others followed suit. We had to reach Patchewara bore by nightfall, as that was the only water before Tooroowatchie, fifty miles away in the dunes. It was last light when the sails of the Patchewara bore appeared ahead, and we hastened toward it much relieved. Our spirits sank as quickly as they had risen, for the bore was dry and long abandoned, a rusted creaky skeleton.

We now faced a dilemma as we had only a couple of days' supply of water left. I had planned to go north by north-west, following the dunes to Tooroowatchie waterhole, a day's march away. But now, if that was dry, or if by some misfortune we missed it, we would not have enough water left to reach Cordillo.

By going north-east, a roundabout route, we should strike water at a couple of supposedly good waterholes the next day. As we were, so to speak, still feeling our way, I decided on this latter and safer course, although longer by one day's march.

The diary tells the story of the following day:

27 July, Wednesday. Headed out 8.30, did little but slog, 27½ miles. Creek after creek dry, bore after bore dry, dam after dam dry. Must get water at Leap Year hole or Bloodwood Well or are in dire straits. Bloody sore feet and backside, will sleep well.

The country was now more sandy and scattered mulga and myall scrub started to appear. The dry creekbeds we crossed every four or five miles were lined by a curious tree with drooping blue-grey leaves and a scaly bark of brilliant red hanging in tatters like a coarse wool. Nugget or Frankie occasionally pointed out the tracks of emu and dingo, and, miles from anywhere, the tracks of a barefoot child. They were a week or more old so we didn't bother to investigate further, but I have often wondered about them since. Frequently on the trip Nugget made an effort to teach me the finer points of tracking; he would point out a track, and I would look at it and reply, for example, 'Dingo!'.

But to him that was not all, it was a big old dingo heading in that direction to water late yesterday afternoon. So in fact it did not mean dingo to him, it meant water in that direction. I remembered once long ago walking through the back streets of Athens hopelessly lost, and not being able to speak more than a couple of words of Greek. There were signposts everywhere but I could not read them, just as there were signs everywhere here in the desert if I could only decipher them. Nugget would show me how a little dust was scattered on top of the pressed print, how the wind last night had blown a little off the sharp edge of the print, how a miniature sand slide in front of one print was still moister than the sand around it, and so on. But it is an art acquired over many years, difficult to pick up overnight, and just as difficult to teach. Paddy once reckoned that Nugget could: 'Track a dirty thought across a dry rock'. It was a pretty fair comment.

That night the dingoes howled all round us, and possibly because of this the camels had wandered far off by dawn. I felt a moment of panic as I realised that without them we were in real trouble, but Nugget found their tracks to the south and we were soon under way. Within hours our objective, Leap Year Bore, came in sight, but after so many disappointments we waited until we could see water before getting too excited. Just as well, as the first sip nearly made Paddy ill. It was salty, and salt bores such as this contain not just common salt (sodium chloride) but magnesium salts which cause diarrhoea and increase water loss. Camels, however, can handle high levels of salinity and drank the briny water with relish. They can drink twenty gallons at a sitting, and the noisy contented slurpings did little to help relieve thirsty men.

Beside the windmill was a thatched grass 'wurlie' or shelter hut held together by wire. Judging by the amount of bird droppings inside, it had not been used by man for a long time.

Earlier in the day Nugget said he had seen 'dust from motor car' ahead, but as that seemed unlikely, and as neither Paddy nor I, with our younger eyes, could make anything out in the distant haze, we forgot about it. But sure enough, up drove a Land Cruiser bearing the emblem of the South Australian Police. As is the custom in those parts, they stopped for a yarn, inquired about our trip and gave us some idea of the terrain ahead. They seemed quite interested in our navigation, asking us exactly where we were, how far we had come, what provisions we had, whether our radio was working and many other questions all in a friendly, conversational sort of way. It was not until weeks later we discovered that the meeting was far from accidental. In fact, having heard of our trip they had set out to locate us, and, if not satisfied with our ability to survive, they had planned to dissuade us from continuing.

We must have satisfied them, however, as they gave us their last and most precious possessions, four nearly cold cans of beer, which we dispatched in an instant, Frankie alone abstaining. I wonder how many white men of his age would have weakened in similar circumstances.

The younger of the two policemen had been engaged in a long animated conversation with Nugget, whose face soon creased in a gleaming, 'Santa Claus' smile. As the Land Cruiser disappeared in a cloud of dust and good wishes on both sides, Nugget told me that the policeman was 'proper number one fella', had addressed him by his correct title ('chilbi', or elder) and spoken to him in his own language! He was obviously deeply touched by this rare courtesy in a white man, so much so that his 'white man's name', was dropped, and he was 'Chilbi' from there on.

We were to find that the police in these remote regions tended to be like these two; good bushmen most of them, with a real interest in the area and the well-being of the isolated inhabitants. Their range of duties is incredible, from postman to fire chief, mechanic to insurance assessor, stock inspector to radio repairer and back to policeman on Saturday nights. A few, admittedly, do not match the task and are just 'doing time' before getting a more civilised posting. But we were sorry to farewell those two at Leap Year Bore.

The country ahead was beautiful, consisting of high red sandhills dotted with green and blue bushes and scattered yellow and white wildflowers here and there. The dunes were interspersed with clay flats covered in Mitchell grass and the occasional dried-up swamp marked by curiously twisted apple gums. Here in these flats the bird life was abundant: finches, silver eyes and flocks of budgerigars were everywhere. But gone are the many great flocks of pigeons which Wills described.

Pretty it was and the going soft, but we had to pace it all the way to Bloodwood Well, for now we were completely out of water, our ration that day having been four mouthfuls per man. The beer, beautiful at the time, had increased our thirst by causing us to urinate more frequently and drying us out further.

The sergeant, the elder of the two police, had warned us that Bloodwood was very hard to find, being in a tiny valley completely surrounded by high dunes. He was right. It was impossible to spot unless you knew exactly where it was as every dune looks like every other and to be on the wrong side of the right dune, and miss the well by fifty yards, is as good as being ten miles off. We need not have worried. By watching the game trails Chilbi took us straight to it, just on dusk, but one look at the salty crust around the tank told us all we needed to know about that water. It was a parched and disappointed team that faced north again just as the sun was setting.

As I walked I settled back into my now constant daydream, a big cascade in the midst of lush jungle, with a deep waterhole beneath it, crystal clear and icy cold. Occasionally there was a beautiful woman in the pool, but more often just me with my enamel mug.

My reverie was shattered by the startled voices of Chilbi and Frankie behind me. They were pointing excitedly to the east, asking questions in rapid Arunda. I looked in that direction and saw a pair of brolga taking off, a large bird seldom seen so far south. But even more interesting was the tiny muddy soak they had taken off from, lying at the base of a gigantic dune. We boiled both billies for hours, and as we drank cup after cup of tea, we filled the water bags for tomorrow trying to filter out as much mud as we could. The diary describes our fare that night as 'mud curry'. Curry powder turned out to be one of the best things to take on the trip.

It's light, it can cover up the taste of mud, not to mention biltong, which gets very boring, or pork, slightly rotten.

By now our camp was in dark shadow, but the last rays of the setting sun were lighting up the crimson dune above us. Chilbi trudged up to the top and disappeared, to return in complete darkness carrying an armful of a weedy plant I had seen growing on a dune further back. I later found out that this bush is the 'Pitchery' plant which, when dried, is smoked or chewed by the Aboriginals as a mild intoxicant. The dunes around the camp protected us from the dreadful winds which howl across the stony plain at night and had had us almost frozen at our last few camps. Even so, the thermometer showed only 2°C at midnight. This wind seemed to cut through blankets and swags to numb our very marrow, and by day it dried and cracked our lips and sunburnt faces.

The next morning we were away at dawn, and, after a few more miles of narrow clay flats weaving below the high dunes, the country gave way to a plain of hard, sharp stones the size of a man's fist. Even in our thick-soled boots it was hellish going, so we were prepared to be pretty understanding about the camels' slower pace.

We had been going a week now from the 'Dig Tree', and it was time to take stock. That kept my mind busy as we carefully stepped our way between the gibbers. First, the camels were performing well in stone which was worse than we had imagined. The equipment was working and in the first week we had covered one hundred and sixteen miles, much of which was bad stone. However, we had been forced by water problems further east than had been expected, adding to the total distance. Far to the west of us, over the other side of the dunes and the flooded Coongie Lakes, was Burke's seventh camp; he had covered a similar distance almost to the mile, and was at that stage in similar country:

Sat. 22 Dec., 1860 . . . We camped at the foot of a sandridge jutting out on the stony desert.

But the stores were not working out as planned. We had counted on living off the land quite a bit, as I felt Burke must have done. However, there was little game about. I was later to discover that there never was an abundance of 'roo or emu in these parts, according to the old records of the early pastoral companies and the pioneers before them. Thus we were eating our dried or salted meat at a high rate, and had left much of it behind anyway. Sugar, which I had planned to use at the rate of one teaspoon per cup of tea, went at half a handful per cup, and many cups we had; billy tea is a great brew for the thirsty and weary.

On the other hand we were falling into a good working routine. Chilbi and Paddy would get up before dawn and set off after the camels while Frankie and I (the sleepy-heads) would boil the billy, roll up the swags and pack away the cooking gear, setting aside the lunch pack and filling up the water bags for the day. This practice is vital, for water in the big metal tanks gets very hot, and by midday is undrinkable. In the canvas water bags the evaporation keeps it cool. As well, without unloading the tanker camel (Wallaper), it is impossible to get more water during the day, thus to forget this task is to incur the wrath of all. Each made his own breakfast, a handful of rolled oats with milk powder and sugar, with a touch of water from the billy. Then all joined in the task of removing the hobbles and 'hushing' down and saddling the camels, loading them up and tying them in line for the day's journey.

Paddy and I took turns at 'dawn walk', an hour-and-a-half stretch, while the other climbed aboard Ginger and navigated. Chilbi on Alice and Frankie on Paddymelon brought up the rear. After the first walk we paused briefly, took off our heavy coats, gloves and balaclavas, rolled a cigarette each and changed over for an hour and a half, followed by hourly changes till lunch. Lunch consisted of a piece of damper, some dried fruit, a cup of effervescent vitamin mix, and a good lie-down for half an hour. Then on the track again, until around five o'clock when we would start scanning ahead for a suitable campsite. We looked for a site which offered good browsing for the camels, handy firewood, a flat stone-free clearing, and, if at all possible, a waterhole.

Once we reached camp the camels were unloaded and hobbled as quickly as possible. While Frankie got the fire going Paddy wrote his day's notes or mended saddlery, Chilbi made the damper and I cooked the main meal of the day, a curry or stew. It was interesting to compare our day's march with Burke's. As they travelled in the height of summer they were forced to break in the middle of the day when the heat was at its worst. When crossing the Stony Desert they had resorted to travelling by moonlight. Their days had started at 4.30 or 5.00 am and they usually travelled for an hour or more before pausing for a quick breakfast break, then continued again until midday, resting for a couple of hours. Burke or Wills generally walked up ahead with the compass while King led the camels and Grey the horse. They rode only when they were tired and generally halted around five, when Wills would write up his diary and occasionally do some astronomical observations while the rations were shared out; a pound of damper and three quarters of a pound of dried horsemeat each with a small piece of pork, and some rice every second day. We had no tents, nor had they, just threw the bedrolls down around the fire, and in fact their camp was probably pretty much like ours, where there was little talk since everyone was tired and lost in his own thoughts. Occasionally I would do a star sighting, but once camp is made and the swag unrolled, any activity is an effort, and any effort not immediately and vitally necessary is dismissed. Mostly we lay on our swags in silence, tea cup in one hand, cigarette in the other, boots off and eyes staring into the warm coals and the drifting wisps of smoke.

Enough detail of Burke's provisions was given in the diaries and told by King later to allow examination of their diet in the light of today's knowledge about man's dietary requirements. The results of that exercise are most enlightening, for their diet contained little or no vitamin C and very little vitamin A. The lack of vitamin C for any length of time produces scurvy, that dreadful disease which Vasco da Gama first experienced when in 1497 he lost one hundred out of one hundred and sixty men, and which had plagued sailors ever after. In 1535 Jacques Cartier's seamen were suffering greatly from the disease when the natives of New-foundland showed them how to cure it by boiling the leaves and bark of a spruce tree and, as reported, 'then to drinke of the sayd decoction every other day, and put the dregs of it upon his legs that is sicke'. It re-putedly worked, but naval surgeon James Lind, in 1747, found an even better cure, citrus fruits such as oranges and lemons. By 1795 British Navy regulations required that each ship be provisioned with citrus juice; and in Burke's day ascorbic acid (vitamin C) was used to prevent outbreaks of the disease. But Burke seemed to have left his ascorbic acid back at Cooper's Creek. The most simple sailor of the day would have gasped at this lunacy. If he managed to return within the twelve weeks he might just avoid the rotten gums, skin sores and the final agonising death characteristic of scurvy.

Our going that morning was some of the worst we had encountered, all sharp young gibber now that the giant red dunes lay behind us. Lar-rikin handled the stone badly—and dragged back. Lunchtime, however, was bliss. Halfway through the pre-lunch stretch we saw a line of trees ahead, big trees, and beyond them more dunes.

On reaching the trees we saw the clear water of the Mariana Waterhole, and our splendid lunch that day was mostly water, but lots of it. I remember sitting on the bank and wondering who Mariana was, what lonely soul thought of her as he gazed into these blue waters. It struck me that a woman is much better immortalised by a beautiful life-giving waterhole like this than by having a busy city street named after her.

After lunch we headed through some of the largest and most beautiful dunes I have ever seen. The country in between was of flat clay, and walk-ing on it was like walking on a newly-rolled tennis court. But, after a few hours the dunes receded to the south, and once again we found ourselves enduring the stone.

On the third walk after lunch Chilbi suddenly pointed ahead and yelled 'Station up there!' Straining our eyes we could make out what appeared to be a radio mast, and even with the glasses it was to be glimpsed only for seconds before disappearing in the dancing heat haze. Cordillo! Our pace quickened as we reckoned it was but a couple of miles away.

They were a long couple of miles. Plain rolled on endlessly and even after the homestead came in sight we walked for hours. A lonelier site for a homestead does not exist—just a rocky knoll rising out of the gibber plains, with only the red dunes far to the south to show that the earth is not one vast sea of stone. But below the rocky knoll lay two huge waterholes, and to these we headed.

The station manager came down and informed us that our camels were to steer clear of the homestead, since horses bolt as soon as they smell them. We were to be told this on many occasions, but in fact we found that, by and large, horses are not in the slightest bit worried by camels; in fact they generally race up and have a good look before trotting off. On one occasion, however, a horse did go berserk at our arrival, but whether or not our camels were responsible I just don't know.

Shortly before we made camp a vehicle appeared and disgorged two men from the National Geographic Society of America, a body which had also contributed to our trip. They were here to photograph us. As we made camp on the bank of the waterhole the extra company instilled a party spirit into our weary team, so we splurged out on a big pork and sultana curry, washed down (somewhat inappropriately) with several bottles of 1972 Tyrrells Cabernet-Sauvignon, courtesy of Joe. Both of our American guests were named Joe, so we nick-named them 'Jo-Jo', and for the next few days as we plodded along the call would suddenly go up, 'Jo-Jo coming!' They were good company, and the talk flowed round the camp fire that night long after the moon was up, until we crawled, tired and contented, into our swags, knowing that tomorrow was a rest day and, mercifully, we could sleep in.

As luck would have it, the camels wandered down to the waterhole for a drink at dawn, and woke the thousands of noisy corellas which perch in the trees along its banks. Thus we were up early, bleary-eyed and somewhat hungover, the billy boiling before Orion faded in the dawn sky. The day passed pleasantly on the thousand-and-one camp chores that wait patiently until rest days. We radioed our position to the Sisters at Birdsville, and back came that reassuring reply: 'November Golf Oscar, receiving you loud and clear. Understand we will see you in seven days. Good luck, over and out'.

Although rarely used and occupying precious space, the portable radio was a treasured possession, our insurance policy, for it meant that in the event of a disaster we could get in touch with Flying Doctor bases anywhere from Broken Hill to the Gulf. Not to have taken it would have been irresponsible, for it costs the people of the outback a lot of time and money looking for idiots who venture unprepared into these parts telling no one where they are going, sometimes paying the ultimate penalty and dying of thirst before they are found.

The people from the station, Lee and John Perry, made us welcome with meat and sugar and advice on the country to the north-west. We nose-pegged Larrikin, rested before consuming grilled steak followed by boiled rice and sugar and were later joined by 'Jo-Jo' and some 'ringers' or stockmen from the station. A 'tailor-made' cigarette, a beer cooled in the creek, and the lively company at the end of the rest day put us in remarkable spirits and we swagged down warmly. My diary recalls what the next day offered.

Sunday, 31st July, 1977. Left Cordillo heading N x NW for Caldega. More and more stone, really bad, a geological junk heap. Stony mountains to the east for variety . . . mirages bad in this region, the rocks start to dance in the corner of one's eye. Down to last 2 'tailor-mades', short on cigarette paper and toilet paper and baking powder for the damper.

It may seem strange, but as soon as the homestead disappeared below the horizon the feeling of solitude set in and the happy company of the last night's camp became nothing more than a distant dream. And it was solitude for, with one leading and one riding, conversation was almost impossible and the few words shouted to each other above the wind only served to underline the silence. Chilbi and Frankie were separated from us not only by the length of the camel train but also by the inevitable barriers of language and culture.

Chilbi's own tongue is Pitjantjatjara, but as Frankie spoke little of this the few words they exchanged in the saddle were in Arunda, a central Australian language which has a gentle timeless quality to it. Paddy spoke a few words of Arunda, and Chilbi a few words of English, and we developed our own 'Patois de voyage', a combination of English, Pitjantjatjara and Arunda.

But that was to come later. For the time being each trod alone across the plain surrounded by stone and his own thoughts. Mine turned to the description 'Stony Desert'. Mike Steele, a bushman who knows these parts well, says he would like someone to show him where 'it' is. There is indeed stone all through this country, but it is frequently interspersed with sand dunes, claypans, swamps, good and well-grassed downs, and, in good seasons, lakes and rivers. It is only in odd spots that one comes upon an unbroken horizon of stone, a fact which Wills remarked on:

We camped at the foot of a sand-ridge jutting out on the stony desert. I was rather disappointed but not altogether surprised, to find the latter nothing more nor less than stony rises that we had before met with, only on a larger scale and not quite as undulating.

Actually the stone country starts as far south as Broken Hill and occurs in patches as far north as the Selwyns, a point we were to appreciate later.

Our trek that day revealed the paucity of wildlife in this country. We saw two dingoes and six hawks in the entire day's march, thus Providence Waterhole was greatly appreciated, surrounded as it was by flocks of budgerigar and quarrians and home for two elegant brolgas. There was a vehicle track of sorts going through to Cadelga, but like all vehicle tracks it followed the high stone country to avoid the clay or sand which become impassable in the wet. We, on the other hand, had no need for more stone, so we headed north, leaving the road far to the east.

We were soon wondering whether we had made a wise decision, as some miles on we found ourselves traversing a series of rocky rises and sharply eroded gullies. The camels took to this terrain with little grace, and both Paddy and I were soon nearing exhaustion coercing the poor beasts as they crawled and slipped up and down the steep slopes. We were in fairly low spirits when the ridges suddenly gave way to a different scene altogether; we flopped down and shared a soothing cigarette as we surveyed a fabulous valley, bounded to the west by high sand dunes and to the east by a low range which ran off the one we had just crossed. Below us the valley floor was broad and flat, a claypan hidden beneath a carpet of wildflowers and in the centre a swamp that was teeming with life. We hurried on.

In the distance herds of emu moved unconcerned by our intrusion, and overhead flight after flight of waterfowl accompanied us. Ahead, a group of ten emus ceased their foraging to watch us approach, then in their own curious way, waddled straight up to us. This incredible lack of fear was evident in all the animals of that valley, a sign man had not been here for a long, long time. But we were hungry for meat, and as Paddy said, 'It might as well have walked straight into our tucker bag'. At almost point blank range, one emu went down. The others scuttled off a few paces, but their curiosity got the better of them, and they came back one by one to within arm's reach until we all stood in a close group, man and emu, watching Chilbi skin our dinner. Our camels took the opportunity to rest, and withstood the closest inspection by the emus with what looked like studied indifference.

I think that if I ever return to that valley I will leave my gun behind, as it almost seemed like a breach of confidence to use it. The emus paddled along beside us when we got under way again, keeping us company until something else caught their interest and they pottered off. They are strange animals, in fact the least graceful birds I have ever seen.

Shortly after the emus departed Frankie yelled and pointed to a green-leafed creeper growing over the clay. Within minutes we were picking handfuls of a green grape-like fruit—the flesh of which tasted remarkably like passionfruit—off these vines. I found the berries delightful and made a splendid lunch of them. It was nearly three hours later when the pains first started, a racking urgent spasm in my abdomen which served to remind me of the shortage of toilet paper. In another fifteen minutes I realised I was in dire straits and did my first aerial dismount, heading for the cover of a small lignum bush a hundred yards away.

The first fifty yards I covered in good style and record time, but the situation became more acute and the last fifty were covered more in the manner of a sack race, with encouragement and loud laughter following me in English, Arunta and Pitjantjatjara. I think those berries could be used medicinally; they are certainly the most effective purgative I have ever known.

Wills had also tried the local fare with unfortunate results:

21st Dec. 1861: I observed . . . two wild plants of the gourd or melon tribe, one much resembling a stunted cucumber, the other, both in leaf and appearance of fruit, was very similar to a small model of watermelon . . . On tasting the pulp of the newly found fruit, which was about the size of a large pea, I found it to be so acid that it was with difficulty that I removed the taste from my mouth.

The valley was now widening out into a dry endless plain with tree lines marking the locations of dry creek beds on the horizon. The heat haze lifted these stunted trees until they appeared to float above the surface like the sails of an old square-rigger. As I rode along I was taken back in time to a trip I once made across the Amboseli plain in Africa, where zebra and giraffe in the distance appeared to be walking about twenty feet above a shimmering silver sea.

In fact the terrain here could have been picked straight out of Africa, and, swaying gently from side to side on the camel, I remember wondering how the explorers in Africa felt. What were they looking for? What drives any explorer for that matter? Alec Chisholm, the President of the Royal Australian Historical Society, once remarked:

> Australia's explorers . . . were a very mixed assortment . . . The chief thing they had in common was devotion to adventuring . . . But a more potent influence was the pursuit of glory. Undoubtedly some of the land explorers had their sights firmly set on fame; and this, one may suggest, was not to their discredit, or at least only mildly so, for in practically every instance it merged with a third and deeper motive . . . the thrill of discovery.

These were certainly the motives of most explorers, but the ratio of adventure-seeking to glory-seeking was different for each. Whereas the daily notes of most explorers are crammed with notes of new plants, animals, and mountain ranges, descriptions of new tribes or cultures, Burke kept no such diary but raced for the Gulf, determined to beat the South Australian expedition. He sought glory, pure and simple. In a letter to his sister he had written: 'I am confident of success, but know that failure is possible; and I know that failure would, to me, be ruin!' He was a glory seeker, and the worst that can befall such a man is to see someone else get the glory. To the west rode the men of Stuart's South Australian expedition, mounted on fast horses, determined to beat Burke's camels.

It must have been a terrible let-down to be a glory seeker in Central Australia. In Africa, John Speke was encountering lush forests and gigantic lakes; other explorers there found new grazing lands, strange tribes or a fortune in ivory. Père David, in Asia, was preparing to trace the fabled bei-shung (panda) to the Hsaifan Mountains of Man-Tzi, closed even to the Chinese for many centuries. In the Americas rich prairies, gold, timber and entire new Indian civilisations greeted the explorer. But in Australia, the further they ventured, the drier it became, each ridge more barren than the last. The continent was, by European standards, a wilderness. There was no city of gold over the next sand dune, just more dunes, and the only reward was the satisfaction of being the first to reach that dune. Those who survived and returned again and again were either dedicated explorers or simply adventurers, men to whom a city office was greater torture than thirst or privation. By contrast, had Burke survived, it is unlikely that the outback would have seen him again.

And yet barren though it is, this landscape offers something else, something hard to define. For in struggling across it like an ant across a gigantic saucer, totally and utterly alone, under the blue dome of the sky, man is struck by the immensity of this land thus and made aware of his own insignificance. It will be there unchanged centuries after he is forgotten. He has discovered not something of glory, but something of eternity.

It is strange how mind and body dissociate from each other under those conditions, for I recall contemplating the mysterious ways of explorers and eternity whilst I stumbled over gibber, smelling of sweat and camel and singing a ditty about an Eskimo lass of ill repute.

Sundown brought us to a line of tall trees running east to west along the banks of an enormous waterhole sixty yards wide and miles long. The trees were alive with millions of corellas and galahs. As we made camp beneath a spreading coolibah we were attacked by swarms of mosquitoes which did not let up all night and were only kept at bay by continually stoking the campfire. Paddy claimed to have lost a couple of pints of blood at the very least.

The night was one of the coldest yet, the thermometer registering 2°C at dawn. We were eleven days and one hundred and ninety miles out from Cooper's Creek, level with, but far to the east of, Burke's camp 75. Since we had a fire going, we breakfasted on fried emu and set out well-fed and confident. Probably it was this feeling of well-being that made me a little lax in my navigation, for we were soon lost. Our map had shown a sizeable creek to the north-east of the waterhole, but we failed to realise that a meagre dry gully we crossed was the 'creek' in question, and so we kept heading north-east towards a line of trees which, as it turned out, marked a large dry swamp. Turning north we trudged through mile after mile of dry swamp and gilgai, rough going indeed, prompting Paddy to question my ability to navigate out of a country dunny.

The swamp stopped abruptly at the foot of a low range, which soon gave way to sand dunes. A cooling breeze sprang up and gently stirred the numerous wildflowers. It was almost worth getting lost to see them. On the shoulder of one of the dunes we picked up the tracks of a vehicle and followed them to Caldega, an old out-station. Built from solid stone, to withstand sieges by the Aboriginals, it now stands in ruins, abandoned by man but host to a number of sleepy lizards which come out from cracks in the stonework to sun themselves.

We had intended to cut west from here, as we were now two hundred miles north of Cooper's Creek, well clear of the floods. But a chance encounter with an old-timer repairing a fence near the ruins convinced us to head north into Queensland, for bad stone lay to the west. He didn't mention the bad stone to the north, so off we headed. Fools!!

The rest of that day was good going, sandhills, claypans and masses of wildflowers, with bees and finches flitting between them. In mid-afternoon we crossed a flat covered with the most peculiar cane grass, so tall it almost obscured the camels. Displaying little hesitation in pushing through it they sampled as they went. Shortly after that a high fence loomed up, the Queensland border. We camped that night on the side of a large dune, and feasted on the remainder of the emu. Sunset that evening was a brilliant purple, and turned the red sand dune a most extraordinary colour.

As we sat round the camp fire that night Chilbi produced his Pitchery, collected back at Bloodwood, and out of curiosity I tried some, rolled into a cigarette with tobacco. The result was a foul taste, cough, headache and insomnia. I don't think the authorities need worry about its catching on with the 'youth of today'.

Our next day's route lay north and across it on the map lay 'The Shallow Lake'. Now lakes in these parts are mostly shallow at the best of times, being bone dry for years on end. Thus I confidently drew our course straight across 'The Shallow Lake'. As it turned out, there really was a lake, deep blue water miles wide surrounded by lush flats and scattered box and eucalypt, with flocks of waterfowl resting on the banks. As we skirted it to the east we were in for another surprise, steep stony escarpments not mentioned on the map. We were to find, as we progressed, that some maps were very reliable, others hopelessly misleading. Even the best are twenty years out of date, since so many wells, bores, roads and stations have been abandoned, fences pulled down and waterholes silted up; but how anyone could miss a gigantic stone breakaway, which has been in the same spot for eternity, was beyond our comprehension.

To the north of the shallow lake (re-christened 'The Bloody Big Deep Lake' by Paddy) we followed a large sand dune until about midday when we crossed the Windorah track, and once again found ourselves on gibber plains. The wind, which had cooled us earlier in the dunes, now ceased, and the heat started to affect men and camels. But at last we saw up ahead the wide green plain of the Diamantina River dancing above the heat haze.

Here, too, we saw a herd of magnificent desert horses going down to water at the river. These animals are bred for the desert and are incredibly hardy, carrying a mixture of brumby, thoroughbred and Arab bloodlines. These and similar horses from other harsh regions (notably the Kimberleys in Western Australia) provided the mounts for the famous Australian Light Horse. It is an amazing sight to watch them whirling across the stone in a cloud of red dust, where the average horse would be lame inside an hour. Wright. who led the relief team from Menindee in 1861, was to remark on the fact that horses bred on the Darling River simply couldn't cope with desert conditions, and this was to be a matter of crucial importance as later events showed.

But I would gladly have swapped Larrikin for any horse that day as he was continually giving trouble, pulling back or breaking file. He even managed to break his nose-peg with a sudden dash to leave the team. By now his condition was the cause of some concern as he had been losing weight rapidly. A year or so earlier he had broken his jaw, and although the bone had mended, it had left the lower jaw slightly out of line with the upper, making it difficult for him to chew. In the country we were going through there was precious little to eat anyway, making his plight so much the worse.

Off to the right we made out the roof of a building nestled in the foot of a large hill, and found it to be a shed with a rain water tank. The water was sweet and cool and we greedily drank our fill. It seems strange that a drink of cold water, a bit of shade and a quiet smoke can give such pleasure, but it is strange only until you have been without for some time. We knew exactly how Burke and Wills felt when they wrote:

Thursday, 20th December: We did not leave this camp until half past 8, having delayed to refill the water bags with the milky water, which all of us found to be a great treat again.

The shed belonged to Durrie Station now visible in the distance but too far out of our way. We set out west again. As we did so a car appeared in a cloud of dust carrying the homestead children to see the camels, and an invitation to eat at the homestead that night. For some reason which I never discovered, Chilbi would not come; perhaps he was just plain tired. Frankie, of course, would not go without him.

We camped about eight miles west of the homestead that night and our host, Jim Evans, arrived to drive us back for tea, bringing with him a couple of large steaks each for Chilbi and Frankie. It was a memorable night, a shower followed by two helpings each of roast beef with gravy, potato, carrots, peas, then lemon sago and custard! Colleen, our hostess, was used to feeding men who had been droving in these parts, and calmly and seriously enquired whether we had had enough.

Over a cup of tea the talk turned to cattle, horses, the droughts, the floods, and the wildlife, and we soon realised that our host was not only a good bushman but a dedicated naturalist who had collected many valuable specimens for museums and research institutions.

Back at camp we slept like logs, dreaming of second helpings of lemon sago. The camels were also thinking of food, for dawn found them miles away amongst the lignum bushes on the Diamantina flats, and we did not break camp until a quarter to nine. Shortly afterwards one of the Aboriginals from the station drove up with a present of cigarettes for Chilbi (which he doesn't smoke, but we did!) and a rolled-up bullock hide. This was so large it was carried across the lap of the lead rider, either Paddy or myself. We found that it made an excellent drum and I am sure that such was the origin of drums: a simple rolled entire hide awaiting use for clothing or whatever.

As the sun rose higher the drumming died down, for the day was fiercely hot, and the gibber as bad as we had yet crossed. We were on the Windorah track now, a trail of gibbers exactly the same as all the surrounds but marked by a white stone or stake at intervals. We trudged on, sticking to our pace, but the miles went past slowly. Nothing moved around us, a state we had come to regard as normal, so that after a while my eyes kept looking at my feet just to watch movement. It was in such a mood, feet shuffling and camel chains clinking in unison, that we encountered the 'Fierce Snake'.

This snake was discovered in 1879 by Frederick McCoy, and at first was thought to be a type of brown snake; later it was called the western taipan. But in recent years research on its venom has shown that this is a distinct species and is undoubtedly Australia's most dangerous snake. What with its somewhat aggressive nature (hence the name), and the fact that the venom is many times more potent than that of a tiger snake or taipan, it is not to be fooled with.

Thus, when Paddy noticed a long glistening shape just a few yards ahead of me we halted to examine (and avoid) the creature. It was about five to six feet long, with a black head and slender bronze body, and it moved out of our way with an unhurried grace, showing none of the behaviour which its name suggests. From then on, however, I made a special effort to keep my eyes off my feet and fix them on the ground a reasonable way ahead. We were to encounter many other snakes on the journey. On one occasion a snake glided between Paddy and the lead camel but neither took the slightest notice. Camels are very phlegmatic.

The heat in that country not only comes down from above, it is also reflected up from the stone below and all of us started to find the going heavy. We saw ahead yet another line of stunted trees in a rocky gully and decided to lunch there. When we reached it we found a delightful little rock hole about six inches deep and it seemed almost too cold to drink. All agreed to pause there for a siesta, but the flies, ants and mosquitoes made sleep impossible. Instead I sat with my feet in the water, wriggling my toes and watching the water-bugs scuttle about; 'boatmen' we used to call them when I was a kid. This pleasant interlude was one which none of us wanted to end; it was a major effort to get ourselves going again. Indeed, so great was the lassitude which set in that we decided, however pleasant it might have been, that we simply could not afford to take siestas in future.

I cannot recall anything that afternoon except stone and heat and flopping exhausted somewhere on the plain that night, too tired even to take my boots off. Needless to say, I slept soundly for we had covered thirty miles which was all that mattered. We were fourteen days and 278 miles out from Cooper's Creek, level with Burke's Camp 78 on the Diamantina, two days' march to the west.

Next morning, we all slept in and, since I woke up with my boots on, I decided to help Chilbi find the camels. In the grey of dawn we set out, and searched for half an hour before we spotted Wallaper kneeling down behind some stunted scrub. Half a mile on we came upon Alice, Sheba and Paddymelon in the scrub of a dry creek, and following this creek we crossed the tracks of Frances, Ginger and Larrikin heading west. Larrikin was in his most murderous mood that morning, lashing out, biting and doing his best to break away. Frankie tried to hold the rest of the camels and keep them calm, and Chilbi and I did our best to hold Larrikin while Paddy fought to hush him down and get his saddle on. Roaring and complaining Larrikin would go down, and when Paddy reached underneath him to pull the girth strap across, he would rear up in an instant and lash out at Paddy or strike at one of us. At one stage he caught me a sharp smack on the hip bone. I think most men would have left him there and then, particularly after he dragged all three of us crashing through a thicket of thornbush and we wound up a tangle of thornbush, ropes, men and angry camel thrashing around in a dry creek bed. But he reckoned without Paddy, who, in his usual determined fashion, kept going straight back in, and eventually mastered the big pack camel.

There are two distinct species of camels, the two-humped 'Bactrian' camel of central Asia and the one-humped 'Dromedary' of India and the Middle East. Only a few Bactrians were ever imported into Australia, but thousands of one-humped camels were brought out for use in our arid regions, and a strain developed here which camel experts contend is equal to the very best Indian types. Just as horsemen will never agree which breed of horse is the best all-round horse, so camel men will argue as to which is the most superior dromedary, the graceful Rajputanas or the sturdy Bikanirs from India or the fine Omai and speedy Hagendowa from the Middle East. Each breed has its supporters, but everyone agrees about Dogla and Thal camels. Of these, one expert simply said 'The Dogla is a mongrel camel, but the Thal is the most miserable of all camels'. Larrikin was behaving like a Dogla-Thal cross that day.

We had lost too much time to sit around over breakfast, so headed off, already stiff and sore from the morning's exertions. No sooner had we started than a fierce wind sprang up from the west, flinging dust and sand in our faces. It was an effort to walk, having to lean into the wind, which was bitterly cold and cut into us like ice. Balaclavas covered our mouths, noses and ears, and gloves and big woolly Bluey coats kept us warm, but we still felt the sting of the sand and the wind as it blew in our faces.

The camels seemed to handle conditions reasonably well, and as I squinted to keep the sand out of my eyes I began to think that in fact camels are pretty well designed for this type of weather. Their nostrils are not round like a horse's, but are long narrow slits full of hair so that they can breathe in a sandstorm without getting a nose full of sand; their eyes are lined with very long thick lashes to keep the sand out, and the ears are small and full of hair, probably for the same reason. As well, their winter wool keeps them warm. A good piece of designing.

The wind kept up, swirling around us as we stopped to eat on top of a large bluff, blowing sand into our lunch of dates, dried figs and damper. The figs I had brought along as a special treat, but only the ants and I had any appreciation of them. After lunch, the two big packers, Larrikin and Wallaper, were acting up, so both Paddy and I had to walk them, riding only for brief spells. Frankie took his turn at the lead, but his short legs and high-heeled riding boots were just not up to the pace.

A few miles after lunch brought a welcome change, for we left the gibber behind and the country we passed through now was lush, well-grassed clayflats, with a tall dune every few miles. The going was good and the wind had now dropped, so we decided to push on to Birdsville which, by my calculations, was only ten or eleven miles away.

But late in the afternoon Larrikin abruptly sat down and refused to budge. By now we were a little concerned about him as his condition had deteriorated markedly. We gave him a couple of injections which he accepted without comment, a bad sign in itself. His load was taken off and packed on to the others; by emptying out most of the water in Wallaper's tanks we lightened him enough to take half the burden; the rest went on to Ginger, which meant one less riding camel. After a half-hour spell, and responding to his lighter load, Larrikin got up and wandered off browsing as if nothing had happened, so we decided he was right to go on.

For an hour all went well, the train moving like clockwork, then abruptly Larrikin fell over. Wallaper, who at one stage had been trained to tow a waggon, simply kept going, towing the poor animal along behind him. Before I had time to halt the team Paddy did an aerial dismount and cut Larrikin's lead rope. He lay quite still for what seemed ages, then slowly righted himself into the kneeling position. He could go no further, the stony desert had taken its toll on us, only six miles short of Birdsville. We were in a broad valley with dunes to the east and west, and the Diamantina River plain to the north. Food and water were plentiful. As he was unlikely to leave this area, we decided to push on, intending to come back for him in a day or two.

By now it was almost dark and Paddy and I together led the team. We were both dog tired and although the setting sun lit up each succeeding dune in a fantastic vista of reds and violets, neither of us had much to say. We just kept walking lost in our own thoughts. I have no doubt that Paddy, like me, was thinking of Larrikin back there. Would he be alright, should Paddy have selected him for the trip, should I have given him some other drug, or given it to him earlier, had he been trying to tell us this morning that he could not go on? Each kept his doubts and feelings quiet and kept on walking.

As the sun finally set we dropped the pace back a little, both for the camels' sakes, and our own, but the camels were reluctant to alter the pace they were used to, and kept bumping us in the dark. Chilbi and Frankie joined us to take the weight off their camels. Perhaps it was due to the day's events we had shared, or a sensation common to any group walking together in the dark, but that was the first time I was to experience the feeling that we were a team, belonging together.

From the top of a particularly high dune the western sky spread before us sprinkled with stars, and off on the horizon, slightly to the north, twinkled the tiny cluster of lights we sought. Birdsville. Two more hours of heartbreaking effort and we were stumbling through the thick scrub

Above: The Digby Peaks, two of the 'three cones' noted by Wills in his diary

Overleaf: Underway on the gibber plains of the Stony Desert—Paddy leading, Tom on Ginger, Larrikin, Wallaper, Francis, Cleo, Nugget on Alice and Frankie on Paddymelon

Border of Mud Camp by Ludwig Becker

which surrounds the river. The moon rose and by its light we wearily unloaded the camels beside a shallow overflow, just south of the village. It was a strange sensation to walk into the old stone pub after nearly three hundred miles of solitude. Everyone seemed to to be talking at once, very loudly. Perhaps they were, as it was Friday night, but in any event it was a grand feeling to sit on a stool and take that first long, cool swig, knowing we had a rest day ahead.

It was Friday, the fifth of August, 1977, fifteen days and three hundred miles from the Cooper, within a mile of Burke and Wills on December 29, 1860. Or so I now thought.

There have been several maps published in historical books showing where Burke and Wills left the Diamantina; some show them leaving it near Birdsville, some fifty miles south of Birdsville and others thirty miles to the east, near the bluff on which we had eaten sandy figs. Which was the actual route?

Throughout western Queensland there are a number of 'Burke and Wills' trees; some with both names carved on them, others with only the initials B-W, and many of them clearly show dates and camp numbers while others are almost indecipherable. Unfortunately, far from assisting anyone to pinpoint the path of the explorers, they serve only to confuse the picture, for the vast majority are fakes, and poor ones at that. King said that the camps were marked only with the letter B, and that only the principal ones were numbered. In addition, anyone who has tried to carve an inscription in a tree will know that it is much easier to carve a Roman numeral, VIII for example, than the modern numeral 8. While Wills refers to his camps by Roman numbers, most of the 'Burke and Wills' trees bear modern numbers. No doubt some of these trees were carved in good faith, by people wanting to mark the position of a guessed or legendary camp, but others are simply the work of pranksters. So to avoid confusion we put no faith in any of them.

While the latitude and longitude of each camp are shown on various maps, they are more often than not miles away from any features such as rivers or mountains which are mentioned in the diary, and thus we had to try and reconstruct their route from the appearance of the countryside as it was described in the expedition's journals.

Wills' entry for the day read:

Field Book No. 3—LAT S. 25½° to 23¾° CAMP LXXVIII to LXXXV. Sunday 30th December, 1860: Finding that the creek was trending considerably towards the east without much likelihood of altering its course, we struck off from it, taking ten days' supply of water, as there were ranges visible to the north, which had the appearance of being stony. A north-east by north course was first taken for about seven miles in order to avoid them.

Thus I was looking for a spot with the following characteristics: it had to be twenty-five-and-a-half degrees south of the equator, on a large creek which lower down runs north-south but turns to the east at this latitude about seven miles south of a stony range. The first possibility, that Burke and Wills had crossed the Diamantina lower down and headed north to Eyre's Creek, meant that this diary entry in fact referred to leaving Eyre's Creek, not the Diamantina. But Eyre's Creek does not turn suddenly east like this, nor is there a mountain range handy. Birdsville has Mount Lewis about seven miles to the north and more ranges to the north-east, and the Diamantina does turn here, but it is almost thirty miles too far south, and Wills, a professional astronomer, would not make an error of that magnitude. So that possibility was out.

The third site, therefore, to the east of my sandy fig bluff, appeared to have been the site. It is on the Diamantina River, only a little to the south of 25½°S. But as we had sat there, flicking ants off our lunch, we had seen no mountains to the north, and no easterly bend in the river. This was not the site either.

Going back to the diary, I thought about our own day's routine, sitting around at night writing up the day's events, taking the star sightings. The answer, when I saw it, was obvious. Wills' diary was written at night and covered that day's going, but gave that night's latitude. Thus they had left the creek that morning, a day's march south of 25½°. Birdsville is twenty-eight miles south of that latitude, a good day's march over alluvial earthy plain. We were actually back on Burke's trail, and right on schedule, but down one camel.

I had time over the next two days to browse through my papers and see how their expedition was faring at this point, one hundred and seventeen years ago. Wills' diary contained only scattered entries, often with gaps of several days between them, so to gain a better idea of their progress we had to fill in the gaps with the odd notes made by King in his journal and the even more cryptic memoranda left by Burke. We had filled some of the remaining blanks through evidence given by King in the enquiry, which took place after the catastrophe, and were thus able to gain a general picture of their progress. They had encountered reasonable good country north-west of Cooper's Creek, Wills describing well-grassed country, box flats, 'valleys ... very pretty, the ground being sound and covered with fresh plants which made them look beautifully green.' They had met with Aboriginals who had given them presents of fish. Burke had been wise to choose this more western course, but it was not without its problems.

They had struck spinifex which Wills called 'porcupine grass'; we were later to discover what he meant by that remark. They also had trouble with the sand dunes of which he said:

We found the ground much worse to travel over than any we have yet met with, as the ridges were exceedingly abrupt and steep on their eastern side, and although sloping gradually towards the west, were so honeycombed in some places by the burrows of rats that the camels were continually in danger of falling.

The point about the rats is interesting, as rats usually build up in large

The Dig Tree

numbers only after a succession of good years. This point, along with the amount of water they encountered, indicates that they travelled in an exceptionally good year. They did strike a fair amount of stone, but it was apparently not too bad going further west, according to Wills.

Having reached one of the lower reaches of the Diamantina on Christmas Eve, they took a day of rest on Grey's Creek to celebrate Christmas. They then made their way up the creek to the Birdsville region. Although Burke did not know it, his back-up organisation was already in trouble. He had left four men behind to establish the depot at Cooper's Creek, and a varied bunch they were at that. In charge was William Brahé, a well-educated young Prussian who had come to Australia to better himself, but who had instead spent eight years as a bullock driver and stockman on a number of outback stations. By all accounts he was an honest, reliable sort of man. With him was Tom McDonough, an Irishman from County Galway, who was a personal friend of Burke, and who could be quite outspoken when he felt the need. Each morning he used to go with Dost Mahommed when he took the camels downstream to graze and would help him bring them back each evening. Dost Mahommed, or Botan, as he was also called, was an Afghan who had accompanied Landells when he brought the camels to Australia. He apparently loved shooting ducks and fishing, but had a morbid fear of the Aboriginals and soon gave up his forays which had added variety to the monotonous diet. The fourth man was William Patten, a tall muscular man as befitted his occupation of blacksmith. Little is known of him but he seems to have been a worrier who normally hid his thoughts behind a bluff, cheery manner. While Botan took the six camels downstream each day, with McDonough to protect him, Patten rode alone upstream with his twelve horses to seek pasture. Brahé remained alone to guard the depot against the Aboriginals who had been crowding around since Burke's departure and who had pilfered several pieces of equipment, which Brahé interpreted as a sign of ill will. A strange little party to face the drudgery of the next few months and to share constant fear of attack by hostile natives, however groundless their fears may have been. When McDonough returned, the two spent each scorching day cutting logs for a stockade to keep the Aboriginals at bay until Wright arrived with the relief party, which was expected any day. But the relief party was far from Cooper's Creek, and Wright was facing his own dilemma back at Menindee, as the following letter shows. It arrived in Melbourne just as Burke and Wills were leaving the Diamantina River where we were now camped.

Depot Camp
Pamamoroo Creek
Darling River NSW
December 19th, 1860.

To the Gentlemen of the Exploration Committee.
Gentlemen,

I have the honor to inform you that, pursuant to a previous understanding with Mr. Burke, it was my intention to rejoin that gentleman, with the members of the party and the stores at present in this camp.

I delayed starting merely because the camels (9) left behind by Mr. Burke were too few in number and too inferior in carrying powers to carry out a really serviceable quantity of provisions. Of horses but seven were left at the depot and of them four are dead, one just dispatched on urgent business, and the remaining two are too poor to be available. When Lyons, the trooper, McPherson, saddler to the expedition, and an Aboriginal started some time back with four of our horses to take on despatches brought by Lyons and represented as urgent, to Mr. Burke, I supposed they would overtake that gentleman at a spot some four hundred miles from here, where Mr. Burke stated to me his intention of remaining some days, and that they would return with all the horses of the advance party, so as to enable me to get out with the stores at the depot.

I regret, however, to have to inform you that the Aboriginal returned to the depot camp yesterday, on foot, greatly exhausted, and that he brought with him a piece of paper, signed by Lyons and McPherson, and imploring immediate assistance to rescue them from imminent starvation.

I have, of course, lost no time in sending out a small party to relieve them, accompanied by the native who brought to me the intelligence of their sad position.

It must be evident, therefore, to the Gentlemen of the Committee, that Mr. Burke has not received the despatches; and that if this season is to be taken advantage of, I can no longer rely upon any horses from the advance party.

As I have every reason to believe that Mr. Burke has pushed on from Cooper's Creek, relying upon finding the depot stores at that watercourse upon his return, there is room for the most serious apprehensions as to the safety of himself and party, should he find that he has miscaculated.

In short, it is my duty to point out to the committee the necessity of the depot stores being at once conveyed to the front.

With the carriage at my disposal it is impossible to effect this, and as I shall require ten horses additional . . .

Burke's change of mind about sending back horses to bring up supplies was now having serious consequences. For the time being, his supply line was cut. Burke, of course, knew nothing of this delay, for he had told Brahé that Wright would be up to relieve him in a few days. Unaware of the ominous turn of events developing behind him, Burke set out north from the Diamantina.

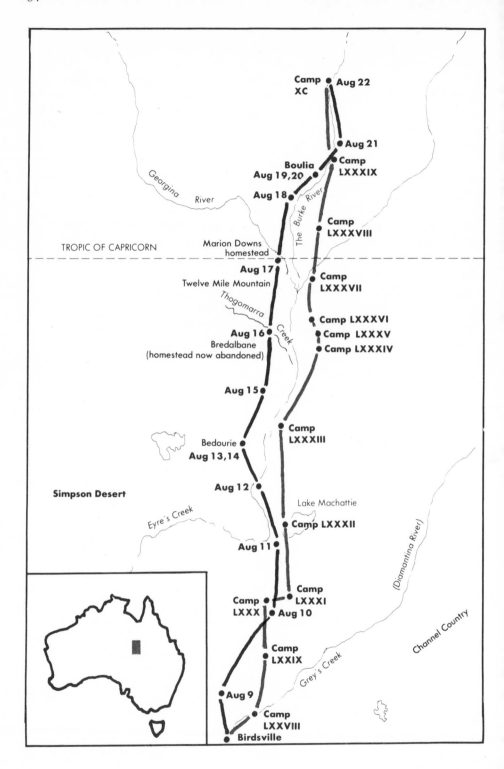

Camp
XC

Aug 22

Aug 21

Camp
LXXXIX

Boulia
Aug 19, 20

Aug 18

Georgina   River

The Burke River

Camp
LXXXVIII

TROPIC OF CAPRICORN

Marion Downs
homestead

Aug 17

Twelve Mile Mountain

Camp
LXXXVII

Thogomarra   Creek

Camp LXXXVI
Camp LXXXV
Camp LXXXIV

Aug 16

Bredalbane
(homestead now abandoned)

Aug 15

Camp
LXXXIII

Bedourie
Aug 13, 14

Simpson Desert

Aug 12

Lake Machattie

Eyre's Creek

Camp LXXXII

Aug 11

(Diamantina River)

Camp
LXXXI

Camp
LXXX

Aug 10

Channel Country

Camp
LXXIX

Grey's Creek

Aug 9

Camp
LXXVIII

Birdsville

THE LAND OF BROWN HAWKS

Birdsville has a population of about sixty people and two million crows, all equally curious about our camp beside the muddy billabong.

The morning was busy with Frankie doing the weekly wash-up and Chilbi and Paddy cutting the bullock hide into strips for hobbles. I was trying to re-pack all the stores so that we could continue with one camel less. Our task was not made any easier by the sightseers wanting us to stop and chat or wanting a ride on the camels so we decided to hobble the camels and let them graze down the creek a bit. But when Frankie tried to find them again late that afternoon they had vanished. Because their feet are flat and soft, camels are quite difficult to track at the best of times,but on a stony riverflat like this it is nearly impossible, so the four of us spread out and went in search of them, Paddy and I going up river and the Aboriginals downstream. After an hour or so of fruitless searching Paddy came to the conclusion that 'the bloody flies have probably eaten them' and we returned to camp. It was a disaster.

I had been re-packing our gear an hour or so earlier, and had left the pack bags open. In our absence the crows had descended in droves and torn to pieces anything they could get hold of: toilet paper, salted bacon, tea, curry powder, and worst of all, navigation charts which were shredded and strewn over the whole clearing. They had even eaten a packet of very potent chilli powder which I hope taught them something.

The loss of the navigation tables was a dreadful blow, for they were vital in determining our exact whereabouts; without them the sextant and computer would be useless. Thus they and about half the medical supplies were left behind to lighten the load. At least, to cheer us up, Chilbi and Frankie returned with the camels.

Following a big stew of 'crows' left-overs' we headed over to the town to see the weekly picture show, which is projected onto a screen beside the road with the viewers sitting in the dust and passing bottles of port around. The film was a badly dubbed Italian Western, and I am not sure whether to blame the port or the scriptwriter but the whole thing was completely incomprehensible. This did not deter the audience, mostly Aboriginal children, who enjoyed it immensely.

The next day Paddy and Chilbi set out for the valley where Larrikin was abandoned, and Frankie and I pottered about the camp cleaning up and attending to the hundreds of tedious little chores that had to be done. The day was hot and still, flies buzzed incessantly and crows circled overhead. I squatted on the muddy bank of the billabong, washing socks that had not been off my feet since Cordillo. They were so bad that Frankie, who had come over to do his washing, moved quietly further down the bank. The offending garments were hung on the nearby lignum bushes to dry, or as Paddy would say, 'for the flies to pick 'em clean'. But when he did return, Paddy was in no mood for jest: he had not been able to find Larrikin. At least we knew that the camel was up and about for circling hawks and crows soon let you know if there is a dead animal in the area.

We had supper that night at the inland mission, a delightful alternative to my cooking, and as our contribution we took along one of Chilbi's dampers. This was a sore point with me, as I pride myself on being a reasonable camp cook, but there is one thing which utterly defeats me, namely damper. Chilbi, on the other hand, turns out beautiful golden loaves every time. I would sit by the camp fire and watch his every move, trying to find the secret. He kneaded the dough carefully, tossed in any amount of salt and baking soda, threw a shovelful of coals into a pit, put the camp oven in, threw earth over it and walked away. Then he would lie back and light up his pipe, totally unconcerned. Later on, at just the right moment (he didn't even have a watch) he would wander over and dig up a perfectly cooked, nicely risen damper. Paddy got the hang of it after a while but I fear that to my dying day I will be turning out dampers that are quite flat, black outside and soggy inside. We had an unspoken understanding that I was to stay away from dampers and concentrate on stews.

Our couple of days had been a pleasant break, and as men and camels seemed to have recovered, it was time to hit the road. We were up at dawn, but the camels had wandered miles down the river again, and by the time we had saddled up and filled the water tanks it was quite late.

The ground was bare and hard, with the sand dunes of the Simpson Desert visible to the west and low rocky ranges ahead and to the east. Although the winds add to them some years, and erode them away in others, the dunes in this part of the world are quite stable and are thought to be about seven thousand years old. In the centre the sand has been packed into a core which makes them fairly solid. They support quite a variety of bushes and shrubs whose greens and olives contrast nicely with the red sand of the dunes, and the grassy clay flats in between support a unique fauna of small birds, reptiles and mammals.

We were keeping an eye open for two birds in particular, both possibly extinct: the night parrot and the scrub wren. Alas, we saw neither, but a month later some friends of mine did re-discover the wren not far from here. We were back into our pace now, a gentle rhythm which has an almost hypnotic effect. The timeless quality of the surrounding countryside somehow enhances this effect; there is no clue as to what century it is, where you are, or who else, if anyone, might have been there before.

It was a rude intrusion therefore when we were greeted by an old Toyota utility which roared up behind us in a cloud of dust and fumes. The driver was a stranger to us, and introduced himself simply as 'Ken from the 'Curry' before telling me that there was an important call from Sydney for me on the radio-telephone back at Birdsville. We were by now about ten miles out so he offered, as people do in these parts, to run me in and bring me back out. As we climbed on board he handed me a can of beer along with an apology because it wasn't too cold. (It was, in fact, just short of boiling.) My heart was in my mouth as we returned, partly because of the driving but mainly because of this 'phone call. I felt instinctively, as any father does, that something terrible had happened to one of the kids.

To make matters worse, when we arrived the radio-telephone was closed down for lunch, and by the time it re-opened an hour later, the Sydney 'party' was out to lunch. After much fretting and worrying on my part the Sydney party came on the air, a journalist wanting to know how we were doing. I told him. In simple, clear, camel driver's language.

My kind driver had not been able to wait any longer and thus I had to accept any lift I could get, in the event a pair of extremely drunk holiday-makers. They drove so fast that it was difficult to see the camel tracks in the fading light, and after a time I could not even make out Paddy's tracks. We drove around aimlessly and it was quite dark before we spotted a tiny twinkle of camp fire in a lignum bush about half a mile to the west. The team had made twenty miles that day despite the late start. Paddy had had to walk nearly all the way and Frankie had walked a good way as well. They were dog tired, and I issued them with a double ration of bacon which I cooked as fast as I could—by the look of them they would have eaten it raw.

My holiday-maker friends decided that this camp life suited them so they pitched tent nearby and infuriated us all by talking 'black-fella' talk to the Aboriginals, which sounded like the gibberish from the Italian Western we had watched recently. It was degrading to hear this fawning, condescending nonsense, and I was about to say something when I caught a glance from Chilbi and noticed the twinkle in his eye. It was all the old man could do to stop himself laughing, but in his most solemn manner he started to utter a few halting words of utter gibberish to their great delight, and so perfectly did he lead them on that I had to retire behind a lignum bush where I found Paddy rolling in stitches of silent laughter, tears running down his face. I broke up completely, and the incident became one of the highlights of our trip. We returned to the campfire to find that one of our guests had fallen in and burnt his hand while the other had trodden on our frying pan and broken it. It was a relief to see them depart the next day.

Just before we rolled into our swags Paddy told me that Frances had a bad sore on her hip bone. The morning light showed that he was right, the extra weight in her packs having worn the skin badly, and so the load was shifted onto Cleo, who had until then been lightly loaded.

We were camped on the edge of a fairly extensive lignum marsh, now dry, and lost quite a bit of time getting out of it and back onto the plain. The going was good for the first twelve miles or so: flat, even clay but with little vegetation beyond scattered tussocks of dead grass, and the occasional mulga or myall tree. We lunched under one of these—damper, dates and biltong again—but lunch over, we had gone but a short way before the country gave way to barren stony downs. Far off on the western horizon a low bleak range was barely visible in the heat haze, and to the east the desert clay plain stretched unbroken as far as the eye could see. The region we were now going through is called the 'Channel Country': a vast desert claypan intersected by broad channels of riverine desert up to twenty miles wide which drain the area. They are of alluvial soil and marked by grasslands with timber lines along the main courseways. This south-western area of Queensland is very dry, and when there is water in these channels it has usually come from heavy falls far to the north and east which may not occur for years on end. But thousands of years ago, before the sand dunes formed, the now dry areas were apparently much better watered as fossils of giant marsh-dwelling kangaroos, turtles and even crocodiles have been found there.

Once, when Nugget had come to stay with me in Sydney, I took him to the Museum and showed him the skeleton of an extinct diprotodon from his tribal area. He just stared and shook his head. It was obviously too difficult for him to conceive the land so familiar to him having been ever any different, populated with such strange, monstrous creatures as this. It was equally difficult for me, walking through the channel country that particular day, to conceive it as a lush marshland. But the country was improving a little as we went, until evening brought us to the ruins of Carcoory homestead, the old stone walls painted crimson by the rays of the sun which was setting far off across the desert.

We set camp at the nearby waterhole, sweet and cool beneath the shading coolibahs. Frankie was relieved of camp duties and sent to catch us a big fat fish, a task he undertook willingly but with no success. It was biltong stew yet again. At least our biltong or 'jerky' was made from beef; Burke made his from horsemeat.

The last torch packed up that night, so the journals and navigation log had to be written by firelight, the glow of which lit up the coolibahs overhead, creating a scene as snug and warm as any living room. As we sat around the dying embers sharing a light night billy, the talk turned to the 'Min-Min' lights which haunt this region. I had been given a firsthand account of this phenomenon by a stockman I met at Birdsville.

The event took place not ten miles south-east of this waterhole, and he told the story like this:

'Bout five year ago, we was bringin' a mob of bullock from Sandringham down to Durrie. We were havin' a bastard of a time shiftin' 'em, they were so bloody poor you could smell their guts through their ribs. Anyhow, we were about ten stragglers down this day so I rode back on me own to pick 'em up. Took me all day to find 'em, and by nightfall I was still a long way out. It woulda been about ten mile south o' Carcoory when I see this light like a car 'eadlight comin' at me. I pulled up about fifty yard short, and then just moved along beside us for a while. Well I rode over and got about 20 yard short o' the bloody thing when it took off, straight past the bullocks so o'course they go in every bloody direction. Bugger 'em, I let 'em go and head for home, but this bloody light comes back and keeps along level with me, even pulls up when I open a gate, or shoots around in front of me at a hundred mile an hour. I was only half a mile short o' camp when it disappeared. Never 'eard any sound, but I can tell yer that horse o' mine saw it too, he was twitchy as hell and shaking all over. Only time I ever seen it, but the blokes from over Muncoonie way reckon they seen 'em lots o' times, and I believe 'em too.

I think he did, too, he was a leathery, down-to-earth sort of a character and only mildly intoxicated at the time.

There have been many such sightings of the 'Min-Min' light in this area, by all sorts of people, both black and white, and somehow they are difficult to explain away as incandescent march-gas, or hallucinations.

Paddy summed the situation up as he rolled into his swag by saying that if any of us saw a 'Min-Min' we should grab it and shove it into the torch so that if it worked we could patent it. With the fire dying and the last of the billy gone we all rolled in, dozing off as the moon came up. We were twenty days and 350 miles from the 'Dig Tree', and five days behind Robert O'Hara Burke. Some time during the night a strong wind came up and the whistling and rustling of the trees woke me up.

Somewhere quite near a small animal was shuffling about, audible in the brief quiet spells between wind gusts. I dozed off again, making a mental note to check for tracks next morning. They were difficult to spot in that hard ground, but Frankie picked them up. There were other similar tracks about, but this was a single set from last night. The tracks were more abundant near a rocky outcrop about half a mile south of the camp, where a number of rabbit-style burrows had been dug. They showed that the animal was a very small member of the kangaroo family, with a long hind foot and a hand-shaped forepaw. It could have been a bettong, now fairly rare, or it may even have been the strange little desert rat kangaroo. Because of the burrow I suspect it was the bettong, but we could not wait around to catch one for a photograph. This was one of the great frustrations of the trip, going through this fascinating country and not being able to pull up and explore the wildlife around us.

But on we pressed, last night's snug camp forgotten already as a barren, treeless plain unfolded in front of us. It was the hottest day we had had yet; both Paddy and I were stripped to the waist by morning break. As he walked along in the lead, hands on hips, head down, I noticed that he was getting quite a tan on. But as the sun rose higher and the sweat started to trickle down his back, quite a lot of his tan ran down with it. None of us had really noticed it, but we had had only one shower in over three hundred miles and the waterholes we had encountered had been too cold to swim or bathe in.

As we came up over a ridge Chilbi let out an excited yell, 'Marloo!! Marloo!!' This meant nothing to me, but looking in the direction they pointed I could just make out the shape of a kangaroo far off to our right. Paddy grabbed the rifle and, crouched double, ran quietly down a shallow gully, coming up to within fifty yards of the 'roo, and despatching it quickly. Fresh meat!

While Paddy had been stalking it the 'roo had moved a little, and something about the way it moved seemed odd to me, so I walked over with Nugget and the tucker bag to check it. On inspecting it I got quite a shock: it was not a kangaroo at all but a large wallaby, with a head and body length of about three and a half feet, and a red head and neck. There are not supposed to be any wallabies in this area, and if this was a red-necked wallaby, as I think it was, then it was at least five hundred miles too far inland. Our luggage problem was such that we carried no preservatives so we could take back no specimens for firm identification. Instead, we cut off both hind legs and tail, put them in a bag on top of Wallaper, had a small sip of water each, and headed off once more, all thinking of meat, fried, grilled or boiled, just fresh meat.

It is strange how necessity can change a person. Here I was, a man whose last trip to the outback was to rescue orphaned joeys and who had spent sleepless nights trying to wean the young animals onto a bottle; now I was drooling over the thought of eating one. It struck me that perhaps all the trappings of 'civilised' man are nothing more than a thin veneer which simply falls away when faced with any primitive drive like fear or hunger.

I was later to come across a passage by the ill-fated explorer Ludwig Leichhardt, who came to almost exactly the same conclusions:

Iguanas, opossums, and birds of all kinds, had for some time past been most gladly consigned to our stewing-pot, neither good, bad, nor indifferent being rejected. The dried kangaroo meat, one of our luxuries, differed very little in flavour from the dried beef, and both, after long stewing, afforded us an excellent broth, to which we generally added a little flour. It is remarkable how soon man becomes indifferent to the niceties of food, and, when all the artificial wants of society have dropped off, the bare necessities of life form the only object of his desires.

But even this was gourmet cooking when compared to the explorer, War-burton, a desperate skeleton in 1873 when he wrote out his recipe for camels:

> The inner portions were first eaten; not the liver and other dainty parts only, but all . . . every single scrap. No shred was passed over. Head, feet, hide, tail all went into the boiling pot. Even the very bones were stewed down for soup, and then broken for the marrow. The flesh was cut into thin flat strips and hung on bushes to dry in the sun. The tough, thick hide was cut up and parboiled. The coarse hair was then scraped off with a knife and the leather-like substance replaced in the pot and stewed until it became like the inside of a carpenter's glue pot, both to the taste and to the smell. The head was soon reduced to a polished skull, tongue, brains and cheeks all having disappeared.

His recipe for the foot is equally appealing:

> Cut the foot off at the hock and scrape and singe as much hair off as time and appetite will allow. Stick the end into glowing coals. Burn it for some considerable time. Then strike it smartly with a tomahawk when, if charred, the sole will come off. Place the foot in a bucket and keep it steadily boiling for thirty-six hours. Then your teeth, if good, will enable you to masticate your long deferred dinner.

On their return journey, already showing signs of fatigue, Wills was to record the passing of a camel with the simple epitaph:

Wednesday, 20th March, 1861—Camp 32R.—Feasting Camp.

And so we, too, pressed on, forcing ourselves to make our twenty-five miles before we pitched our 'Feasting Camp'.

By mid-afternoon it was still fiercely hot on the barren plains, and the heat haze and mirages had become worse than ever before. At the change-over, as we both sat resting our backs against the lead camel, Paddy and I shared a cigarette. We generally said little on such occasions as there was little to say. Paddy's eyes were red slits in a face smeared with dust and sweat, and he remarked as he got up to take the lead rope that either he was going blind or that mirage over to the west was real. A casual glance towards it as Ginger lurched up showed a mirage of a vast lake, stretching for miles. But after an hour's going it was still there, and seemed to stretch straight across our path. He had me wondering now, so I pulled out the map and did a few quick calculations.

We had started from Carcoory at 8.15 am, after looking for kangaroo-rats, and had lost half an hour stalking and skinning the 'roo, and half an hour for lunch, thus we had been going for six and a half hours, and had therefore come about nineteen or twenty miles north. The map of that region showed two gigantic lakes ahead, one some miles to our left and the other far away on our right. They were linked on the map by a stream which ran across our path about three miles ahead. I was not yet entirely convinced, we had camped on the dry beds of a couple of 'lakes' already. But slowly it dawned on us that we were approaching some sort of watercourse, for the countryside was changing with each step, and a profusion of wildflowers, lignum and verbena closed in around us. As we pushed through this the noise of our arrival on the stream set off a massed flutter of wings as hundreds and hundreds of waterfowl took to the air. Nearby on the river flat a herd of fat herefords grazed contentedly, barely pausing to watch us pass. Butterflies hovered over the golden wildflowers and flocks of finches and silvereyes flitted from bush to bush heralding our arrival.

We had not quite made our miles yet, but a spot such as this was too good to miss, so we made camp beside a large pool in the fast-moving river. The water was fairly clear, and the large number of pelicans paddling majestically along it indicated an abundance of fish.

Chilbi relieved me of cooking duties, as Marloo was one of his specialities and so, while Frankie tried unsuccessfully again for big fat fish, I wandered downstream for a bath. The water was freezing cold and bracing and to climb into clean clothes smelling of soap was almost sensuous.

During this operation I was subject to the inquisitive stares of a large rookery of spoonbills and ibis, and honked at by a passing pink-eared duck with her brood. After the desert, this spot, Koolivoo, was the most idyllic oasis one could hope for and the smell of roasting meat back at camp was tantalising. With Paddy out after duck and Frankie fishing, we had expectations of even better things to come, but were none too upset when we finally had to make do with what we had. It was delicious, and when we were all so full we could eat no more, we still had the tail left to have cold for lunch the next day.

A twilight stroll through the surrounding bush revealed that there were many waterholes, each teeming with life and fed by numerous fast-flowing streams. The banks were lined with river red gums and thick tangled lignum bush, which our camels were munching with delight.

Since we cut north from the Diamantina we had been following Burke's route fairly closely, but he had had very different adventures here in 1861. King describes an incident on New Year's Day, of that year, on a waterhole in this region.

When we were at breakfast 15 strong able looking Blacks came within 30 yards of our camp led by an elderly man they all had spear & boomerangs the leaders spear was about 25 foot long the others were short then once they made signs to us to leave the place Mr. Burke went up to them & gave some beads and other presents to them thinking they would go when they receive them but they began worse than before

The leader advancing in front sticking his long spear in the earth then taking a handful sand first rubbing his hands with it & then the spear The others following up closely until then we took but little notice of them

Mr. Burke ordered us to get ready our revolvers & ammunition

We got them together when a shot was fired over their heads they ran off a hundred yards

The leader encouraging the remainder to follow up they came again within 40 yards of us when Mr. Burke ordered us all to fire over their heads

Off they ran we saw no more of them until evening when they came again & gave us nets & slings in exchange for a few matches.

From here they pushed on over the stony desert again as we did. In 1861 this region was a far cry from the oasis on which we camped, for it was then bone dry. 'Mud plains,' King complained. 'Nothing to be seen not even a bush we pushed that day making 51 miles & nothing to be seen but mud plains.'

The dawn chorus of the waterfowl woke us from a deep sleep next morning and for a while we just lay in our swags watching the flocks circling, banking, and skimming the surface of the waterhole, some settling, some squabbling, as others took off.

Finally we dragged ourselves out of our swags and were just getting changed when a flock of ducks swam past not thirty feet from where I stood. By the time I had the rifle loaded they had moved off a way, but I managed to hit one, and thought I hit another, for it 'limped' along upstream. I have a deep loathing of anything wounded being left to suffer and so I raced up along the bank stumbling and falling through thick lignum scrub without a stitch on, the 'wounded' bird keeping just ahead all the way. Finally I reached the end of the island on which we were camped and had to dive in after it. The water was freezing, and on surfacing I saw the bird double back the way it had come. Paddy joined the chase by diving in ahead of it, whereupon it took off quite happily, leaving us both to return to camp, naked and wet, blue with cold and (almost) empty handed. We were greeted with a cup of tea and many derisive remarks by the others.

We warmed up as we walked, the circulation slowly returning to fingers and toes. It was a beautiful morning as we moved across the valley, through mile after mile of green meadow sprinkled with golden flowers, and we noticed a number of little black and gold birds which I have not seen before or since. As well, we saw our first bustard or plains turkey. They are a good-sized bird and supposed to be excellent eating, but we did not shoot any as they are protected. Besides, they were very wary of us and as soon as they saw us coming they moved well out of rifle-range and temptation's way.

Many people I spoke to in those parts tell me that although you cannot get near these birds on horseback or on foot they can be approached easily by car. I asked one character up north if he realised that they were protected. 'The only ones protected up here are the ones with a Wildlife Ranger in front of 'em, mate.' We were to encounter the bustard a lot from here on, so that although they were severely reduced at one stage, they seem to be making a comeback in these parts, evidently because not everyone shared that man's outlook.

We were back on the gilgai downs again by lunchtime, and pulled up under a solitary stunted eucalypt. Out came the cups, waterbags, dried dates and damper, but no kangaroo tail. 'Where's the bloody 'roo tail?' I asked. There were quick, embarrassed glances exchanged, then Chilbi spoke up; he had eaten it as we rode along that morning. I had some sharp words to say on the subject of sharing, and our lunch of damper and dates was finished in a heavy silence.

I was re-adjusting one of the packs on Cleo just before we remounted, when Chilbi came and asked what was the name of the next settlement. 'Bedourie', I said. 'Well, boss, I think I better finish up there,' he said. Paddy came over, and between us we managed to convince him that it was not that important, just as long as it didn't happen again.

Things calmed down, but it was now an uneasy camp; a division had fallen between black and white. Although it was a trivial incident, in retrospect, it had served to bring to the surface feelings which had built up gradually over the trip. I had come to prove a point and knew that in doing so we would have to go like hell to average twenty-five miles a day, or better. So I knew from the start what I was in for. Paddy had, I believe, come initially out of a sense of duty to his brother, Greg, but, once committed, he had thrown himself into things from the start, accepting the trip as a challenge and an adventure. We two had shared all the walking, and much of the camp work between us. If two men on their own split the work in half, all is well, but if two others look on, then there is bound to be trouble.

Why had the Aboriginals agreed to come? Chilbi, since he was getting very little pay, had probably come partly to get away from the routine of mission life, partly to 'break-in' young Frankie on the threshold of manhood, and partly because he too had been a friend of Greg's. There was no doubt that both Chilbi and Frankie lacked the motivation to do the trip the way we were doing it, but then they had never avowed to do what we were doing, merely to act as guides. It was a situation which needs time to work itself out, one way or another.

We marched in silence all afternoon, our track winding up over high dunes or running along in the gullies between them. Finally nightfall came when we were still in dune country, miles from any surface water, so we camped on the side of a large sandhill. The long walk had eased the tension a little, and everyone got a good and equal share of roast duck to show that there were no hard feelings.

But later I lay awake, staring up at the stars and wondering about us, and about the Aboriginal peoples generally, for it seemed that our cultures were so far apart. To me it seemed that the European outlook developed in a fertile environment where the crops grown in spring and summer had to be harvested and stored for use over the cold winter. Our

Above: The Monument

Overleaf: Border of the Mud Desert near Desolation Camp by Ludwig Becker

Following: 'Nose-pegging' Ginger
The nose-peg and pegging stick

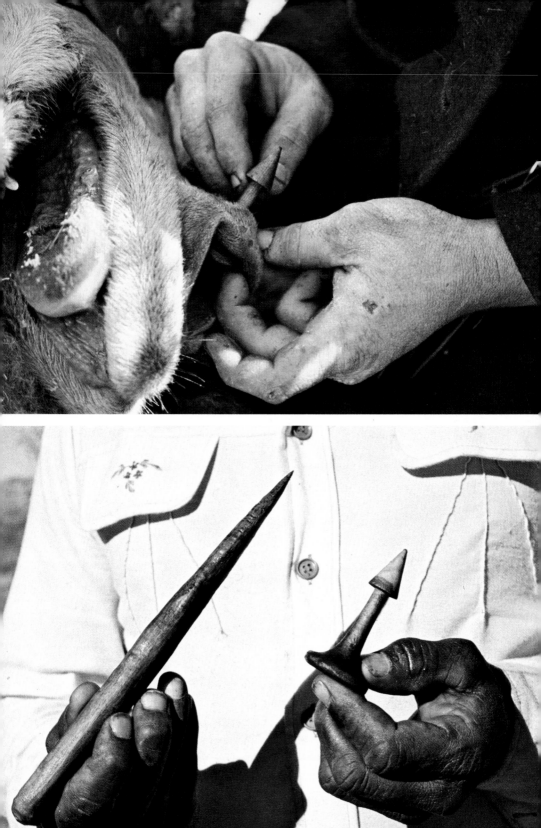

culture therefore is based on the principle of 'he who works hardest plants more, harvests more, stores more, and he and his family will live better in the next winter'. Thus, as Paddy and I did, we throw ourselves into things to produce enough to eat tomorrow and the day after. (Just like the 'roo tail.)

But the Pitjantjatjara face different problems, for their world is hot, dry and barren, and the years bring no reliable alternation of good and bad seasons. There are few plants which could be harvested in large enough quantities to put much aside for tomorrow. There are no beasts of burden and Australian animals are small and few, and lacking in energy-rich fat. Meat does not keep well in this climate. Thus, the Aboriginals developed a culture suitable to a barren land, getting just enough for today, then saving energy. Any excess work will waste precious energy and sweat, both energy and water being scarce commodities. Storage is pointless, as when the waterhole dries up, the tribe must move on, carrying everything with them.

Had our culture evolved in this country, it would have been very similar to theirs, and our outlook, on a venture like this, would, no doubt, be similar. It was upsetting, however, that in our party, the two peoples, each acting true to their values, had been thrown into conflict. I tossed and turned and finally, giving sleep away, stirred the fire for another billy as I mulled over Burke's experiences.

One of his main flaws was his inability to manage men. His second-in-charge, George Landells, and his foreman, Charles Ferguson, had both been sacked at Menindee, and the Doctor also resigned at that time. Dr Beckler's words at the Enquiry floated through my mind:

'It was Mr Burke himself who interfered very often with me . . . which at the time I sent in my resignation I pointed out as one of the reasons.' (Dr Beckler had been in charge of stores.) Besides one of the reasons for my resignation I gave was that Mr Landells had resigned and there was nobody in my opinion sufficiently acquainted with the habits and travelling of camels but Mr Landells himself.'

The Chairman of the Commission of Enquiry: 'In consequence of Mr Landell's resignation you entertained doubt as to the success of the expedition?'

Dr Beckler: 'I did so.'

The Chairman then asked if this was the prime reason. 'No', replied Beckler, 'the prime motive was the treatment which Mr Landells had from Mr Burke . . .'

I looked across the fire at Paddy, our camel-man, and wondered what he thought of my 'man-managment' today, and at Chilbi and Frankie curled up together right next to the fire as is their people's way. Could they understand the clash of the two cultures, or did they simply have a mad leader who got angry over perfectly normal things?

Off to the west somewhere a dingo called, making me feel very lonely sitting by myself on the side of the dune. I thought of home and of the family sitting round the fire—but they would all be snug in bed by now. The thought of snug beds made me realise how cold it had become. I rolled into my swag and dozed off thinking of the kids and watching Alchernar sinking low in the southern sky.

Before too long it was the start of another day and with it the start of a new relationship between us all. Frankie had the fire going and the camp all ship-shape, Chilbi had the camels back from their night's grazing on a distant dune, and they were half packed as I awoke. I had not been sitting alone last night: Nugget showed me the tracks of a big dingo, pointing out the spot not twenty feet away where he had crouched watching me, then the tracks where he came right into camp, probably soon after I hit the swag.

As I peered at the tracks in the sand to try and figure out how he could tell the age of the tracks, I noticed something of equal interest, the silver wrapper from a powerful pain-killing anti-arthritic drug, unlike anything we carried. It emerged that Chilbi had seriously hurt his right knee in a fall from a horse several years ago and that the injury was being badly aggravated by the trip. The sister at Birdsville had given him tablets on the advice of the Flying Doctor. He had not wanted to worry me about it.

We set off across a wide plain of wildflowers with me feeling like a martinet. The flowers were not scattered but formed a solid mass of gold. The soil here was of a rich, black, loamy texture cracked into wide fissures by the scorching heat. We passed the carcass of a cow which the dingoes had killed while she was calving. A thousand crows were now feasting unconcerned by our passing. One of the first things a stranger is likely to notice out here is the almost complete lack of odours. No exhaust fumes, perfumes, gas leaks or garbage. Only the sick-sweet smell of the occasional carcass breaks the monotony. We found that this lack of noises, odours or movement heightens the senses incredibly. In the city, people can live right on a main road and be completely unaware of the noise of a thousand cars, but put that same person out here, and he will re-tune his senses to hear a car ten miles away, or pick out the glint of sun on moving metal. Yet, while the senses are tuned to a high pitch by this vacuum, the brain is dulled by inactivity, and I recall feeling completely and utterly bored that day, and having exhausted all conceivable thought, I wrote '. . . I think I have sung every song I ever knew, whistled every tune ever written'.

We were, by now, living a very simple life, little more advanced than that of animals: up at dawn, walking at an even pace all day, eating whatever happened to turn up, finding a tree to sleep under when the sun went down. Such a lifestyle requires no more mental process than that of a migrating gnu, and in my opinion that is why gnus never developed any further. It is probably also why my mind was becoming less active, like a car left idling too long. Odd, vague thoughts on this point or that gathered like frail clouds and then dispersed again without forming any definite conclusions.

It was obviously the same for Paddy, whose choice of songs was, if anything even more limited than mine, perhaps we were just getting on each other's nerves in this silence. We were, in addition, very tired, and the appearance of a large, stationary dust cloud low on the northern horizon failed to spur us on to any great exertion, we just kept plodding on. It turned out to be a mob of a thousand bullocks plodding equally aimlessly south to find new grazing land, as the country 'up the top end' was getting pretty dry.

The head drover rode over on a fine grey hack which at first looked on the verge of bolting as it was extremely nervous of the camels. But after five minutes it was riding right beside us, even sniffing the camels, so the theory of camels spooking horses took another tumble. The drover rode with us for half an hour as we passed the slowly moving herd and the talk drifted from camels to horses, waterholes to droughts, saddles and back to camels. There is a ritual which is gone through in any such encounter in the bush, a ritual which is as polite and formal (despite the language) as any encountered at an occasion at Government House. Certain topics are compulsory; your health, the weather, your destination, and whether or not you have sufficient meat and water. Any real sign of curiosity is regarded as prying and topics such as politics, religion or current affairs are taboo.

It is quite amusing to listen to a stockman going through this polite litany when it is obvious that he has never seen a camel and is dying to find out all about them, but is prevented by good manners from bombarding you with questions.

He farewelled us as we left the plain and headed through a wide channel of soft alluvial sand which was hard going, even for the camels. Beyond this was a magnificent old dune which ran as straight as a die for five or so miles. Just at the foot of a dune, on each side, there is generally an area of well-packed clay and soil, which, providing the dune is pointing in the right direction, is good going. This one was, and we rushed along at a good rate, covering the twenty-two miles to Bedourie by 2.30 pm. We set camp in a deep gully running off Eyre's Creek, a mile or so south of the tiny outpost. This consisted of a two-room pub and a couple of ramshackle houses.

After unloading we made our way to the hotel, stumbling through the gilgais hidden beneath the long grass. The pub seemed pitch dark after the glare of the sun, and quite cool by comparison; the steady buzz of flies and the 'cra-cra' of crows outside was muted by the stone walls to a quiet murmur in the distance. We were the only customers and, sensing no desire for conversation on the part of the proprietor, we contented ourselves with reading faded race-meeting posters as we sipped the lukewarm beer. It seemed that man had not managed to do a lot with this place since Burke and Wills passed through. It had that defeated air about it, the sort of place where anyone with any get-up-and go has got up and gone, leaving behind only those who cannot, for whatever reason, make the break. Or perhaps it is the remoteness of the place and the harshness of the region which defeats men, for few human ventures can withstand year upon year of drought, followed by massive floods which sweep down on a front many miles wide, casting the debris of fences and dreams high up on the side of the dunes. We bought a bottle of beer each and wandered back to camp to treat the camels before nightfall.

Frances had a bad packsore over the point of her hip bone, which proved to be even worse than I thought, having developed into an abscess beneath the thick woolly fleece. She was not at all co-operative when being treated, in contrast to Wallaper who sat quietly as I treated a pack-gall over his rib cage where the back of the water tank had been rubbing. Remedies for these pack-galls are as many and varied as cures for the common cold. The Bedouin tribes rub a mixture of camel urine and pigeon manure into them, but as pigeons are not always available I had sought an alternative cure. An Afghan from Alice Springs, over eighty years old, once gave me a recipe for treating pack-galls: a mixture of sulphate of zinc and lead acetate which apparently dated back to the time of the Pharaohs, prompting us to nickname it 'Pharaoh's brew'. Surely though, I thought, there must be something more advanced than this. I checked with John Keep, the Professor of Veterinary Medicine at Sydney University, who laughed when he heard this. 'That's almost the exact recipe for white lotion,' he said. 'Used a lot of it on the army remounts during the war. Good stuff it is, too. Most human skin lotions in use today are based on it; zinc creams and calamine lotions for instance.'

So the Pharaohs were not stupid after all, but it seems strange that nearby tribes still swear by camel urine and pigeon manure; perhaps this too should be researched. We used 'Pharaoh's brew' to be safe.

As the next day was to be an R and R day (for rest and repairs), we were to have a big treat for dinner that night with bacon, dried peas and beer. The bacon was by now covered in green mould and smelling decidedly off, but we had found that by cutting off the outside it was still possible to eat the inner parts. Even after a thorough cooking, however, the inside bacon still tasted mouldy, and I was lucky that the warmish beer rinsed out the rancid after-taste. It was a cold night and the sky was so incredibly clear that even the dimmest stars were quite visible, Antares glowing brightly through the leaves of the red gum directly above us and Deneb showing clearly out over the western desert. A breeze sprang up just before turned in, dropping the temperature several degrees. Since we were camped in long dry grass we could risk only the smallest of fires, and we spent a restless, chilly night.

Morning brought with it an exciting discovery. While we were walking up to the outpost the previous day we had noticed a grove of date palms some hundred yards to our left, but had not remarked on it. However, in the light of dawn steam could be seen rising up through the palm trees in the cold morning air. It was an eerie sight and we wandered over to investigate, coming to a halt on the bank of a pool, large, deep and sapphire blue, with wisps of steam rising off the surface. We raced back to camp and returned with towels and soap, tripping over half-off trousers in the process and shivering naked as we picked our way to the water's edge. As we dived in, the water closed over us, so soft and warm that we wanted to stay there forever.

Frankie surfaced with a shriek of joy, his ebony face alight with glee as he dived and splashed like a playful dolphin. When he paused for air he would float for a minute or two, eyes closed and teeth gleaming in a smile of pure ecstasy. The pool was quite deep, and a variety of peculiar algae coated the bottom like a patchwork quilt. The water was crystal clear and heavy with mineral salts, the heat penetrating and soothing weary muscles, gradually relaxing the whole body and lulling the mind into gentle oblivion. It was a delightful place to float half asleep and watching the steam rise up past the date palms, but we had to make practical use of this opportunity as well, and so proceeded to wash clean the foulest collection of clothes I have ever smelled. This was followed by breakfast of bacon and several billies of tea before the inevitable chores were allotted: a new headstall to be made; two sets of hobbles needed; a pack bag to be sewn up; radio to be set up and tested; maps for the next leg to be dug out; the old ones put away (with waterholes marked for the return trip); dishes to be washed and so on.

Fresh from our morning's swim we worked non-stop through the heat of the day and by mid-afternoon we stood back, hot and sweating, to survey the results of our labours. Satisfied, we turned our attention to treating Frances' pack-sores, a task which needed all hands: one to hold her head down; two to lie on top and hold the leg-ropes; and one to treat the wound. She was not a good patient,our Frances; not vicious but nervous and prone to panic. Whereas Wallaper would take a long time to figure out what to do in a given situation and remain immobile while the process of thinking took place, Frances would go straight into it, generally going on the wrong side of a tree, or up the steepest part of any slope. Her saving grace was her stamina, for although she was rangy and only of medium height, she could carry a heavy load with the best. Still, when really bothered, she could kick with the best of them, too.

The ordeal over, we all trudged over to the artesian spring for an afternoon dip but were sadly let down for, although delightful in the freezing dawn, it was too hot to refresh sweaty men in the heat of the afternoon, and was now surrounded by clouds of hungry mosquitoes. We were hurried into getting dressed again by Chilbi muttering 'Kwara coming'.

Two local Aboriginal women wandered up, accompanied by their children, and we all moved off leaving the mosquitoes in charge of the springs. The women treated Chilbi with great respect, as indeed nearly all Aboriginals did on our trip. They obviously had little to eat themselves and joined us in our afternoon treat of dried fruit, meat and damper, gratefully accepting some tea and cigarettes while Paddy, hot and tired though he was, gave each of the children a ride on Black Alice.

They came back late in the afternoon, and brought us bread and jam, which Chilbi accepted as if they had given him the Crown Jewels. They could ill afford to spare the food, but he knew it would have been very bad manners to refuse and he also accepted their invitation to dinner.

That night Paddy decided to stay in camp with Frankie who had not been included in the dinner invitation, so stumbling through the Mitchell grass and gilgais in the dark, Chilbi and I made our way across to the outpost. As we entered the tiny pub a lively scene greeted us this time, at least ten people crowded the bar for the Saturday night get-together.

We were soon engaged in conversation with a couple of stockmen from one of the outlying stations who, true to form, avoided asking about our strange venture until all the preliminary remarks about the weather and so on had been thoroughly dealt with. The talk drifted to the wild animals of the region and one stockman mentioned that he had a brother on Durrie Station who was an authority on the subject, none other than our old friend Jim Evans! When I revealed this tenuous acquaintance I was accepted as a long lost brother.

Chilbi went off to his supper and the crowd thinned somewhat, leaving a half dozen of us to chew the cud round the big log fire. The talk flowed back and forth; stories of broken axles followed talk of floods; good cattle dogs were topped by good stock horses; dingoes shot at a thousand yards bettered by ones shot at two thousand. The firelight flickered across the faces which gazed into it, each story bringing back distant memories to the other faces, either softening them into a smile or striking a sad note, the face drawing tight and closing up.

One woman recalled arriving here as a young girl sitting beside her parents in a buckboard on the long haul up the Birdsville Track. She recounted those long ago days wistfully, remembering how they kept the shotgun loaded as the long trains of the Afghan camel teams approached. Another told of his mother, long buried, who used to go out and barter with the 'Ghans, while his father and brother stayed in the house, covering her with rifles. I began to realise that I had been hasty in the judgment of the people here. Some were drop-outs, true, but the rest were determined bushmen who would not swap this hard life for any other and who are content to live much as the pioneers did.

The talk drifted to the trip I was doing; the possibility that I was bloody mad was mentioned several times, and also that I was too far to the west, since the Aboriginals over on Pallico Channel used to tell of Burke's camping there. They may have been right too, but it was hard to be definite as Wills' and King's statements conflict on their route through here.

The mention of the old Pallico tribe brought up the subject of the Aboriginals, obviously a hot topic in this area, and I noticed that the only person present with any Aboriginal blood in him went out and busied himself getting more firewood during the discussion. Opinions varied somewhat, but all seemed to agree that the 'bloody do-gooders from down in the cities' had 'buggered things up completely'. It seemed that when the first settlers arrived, not long after the country was opened up by Burke and Wills, there had been some pretty bloody skirmishes between black and white. However, the younger Aboriginals eventually drifted into the stations, accepting work as stockmen or housemaids. They were soon followed by their relatives, parents, brothers, sisters, cousins and all, who generally camped a mile or two away from the homestead, but were given (somewhat reluctantly at times) meat, flour, cloth, and, when necessary, medical attention, by the station managers.

This worked out well for the stations, as they paid the Aboriginal workers very little compared to white wages, the savings being, of course, only partly depleted by the cost of killing an extra bullock or two to feed the tribe. The tribe, as long as it stayed, provided a cheap source of extra labour for busy times such as mustering. This led to a somewhat patronising attitude towards the Aboriginals, but they, on their part, did obtain some benefit from such an arrangement. They were able to live together as a people and thus retain some of their tribal identity, some of their customs, and feel that even if they were not treated as equals they were needed and accepted, and to some extent cared for.

The money that the workers earned was used by all to provide the few luxuries obtainable in these parts (rum, blankets, a trip to town and so on), the necessities being provided by the station. But then apparently the 'Ignorant Bloody Southerners' stepped in, and granted 'equal pay for Aboriginals'. It had been well meant, and done in a spirit of equality for all, but around here it spelt disaster.

The unfortunate fact was that the 'equal pay' ruling was brought in at a time when beef prices were falling and wages and costs rising. Thus it suddenly became cheaper for the properties to take on a single young white man than to employ an Aboriginal and support his family. So, from being the backbone of the cattle industry they became unemployable, many drifting into shanty towns, and living on the child endowment and unemployment cheques. With nothing else to do and no prospects for a future, quite a few of them passed the days (and the dole cheques) on drink. Hearing of the plight of the Aboriginals in the north, the government had 'rectified' it by handing out bigger cheques and benefits, only to make the situation worse.

'Could not the Aboriginals be given back the land, or at least enough land for them to become self-sufficient?' I asked.

'Wouldn't do 'em much good, now,' I was told.

The main tribal camps had been sited on the most permanent, reliable water-hole in each region. When the stations were established, or a township built, these prime sites were invariably commandeered, and most other waterholes were not reliable enough to live on. In addition, the overgrazing by cattle and scrub-cutting in drought years had altered the country to such an extent that it would be very hard to live off the land in the traditional sense. Even if they had the funds to set up a cattle venture on the land, the industry is in such a shaky state that it would probably fail.

The future, I was told, looks grim. This train of thought was interrupted by the arrival of the men's wives and children, happy and smiling after a party. Most of the men who had just been talking were married to Aboriginal women and their children generally had Aboriginal features, so their interest in the plight of these people was understandable.

Chilbi returned soon afterwards, and we pulled our coats up around us before trudging back through the long grass to the far-off glow of the campfire. The others were already asleep and Paddy was snoring softly as we crept into our swags and fell asleep.

Dawn brought with it a gentle breeze which stirred the grass around us while we marched. As we passed north of the outpost a very excited stallion raced up to meet us, then veered off again at a gallop, pulling up breathtaking inches short of a high barbed-wire fence. He repeated this manoeuvre a number of times, becoming more agitated each time, and had us quite worried that he would wind up entangled in the loose wire, but finally with a snort of contempt he disappeared.

We headed north, moving along the foot of a majestic dune which ran for mile after mile. To the east the country spread out into flat riverine desert, its surface pitted and cracked, and the monotony relieved here and there by treelines marking seasonal creekbeds. The going was good; firm ground and gentle breeze with both the camels and ourselves picking up the stride of the march. The miles rolled past. Coasting along on Ginger, I had that marvellous sensation of being on a sailing boat again, moving in a light breeze.

After lunch things took a different turn; the breeze dropped and Cleo started to pull back, halting progress every few hundred yards. Finally she was taken out of the number two position and tied on at the rear, Frances being promoted to number two. This improved matters only a little, and it was hard, hot work, the going rougher now that we were on the western flat of the Eyre Creek flood plain. By 4.30 pm we were dog tired, and seeing tall timber not far to the east we made for it, to discover a fine pool of water at the foot of very high steep banks. We decided to camp early and checked out each of the camels.

Cleo appeared to have lost condition a little, and was stonesore on the heel of her right foreleg. The pack sore on Frances had almost healed, but Wallaper had lost all his 'puppy fat', the sinew and muscle noticeable below the skin. Checking the stores we found that the sugar supply in our fortnight's ration kit was almost gone. We unpacked the transceiver and set the aerial up for a routine test:

THIS IS NINE, NOVEMBER GOLF OSCAR, TEST TRANSMITTING ON TWO ZERO TWO ZERO. ANY STATION RECEIVING PLEASE ACKNOWLEDGE, REPEATING, THIS IS NINE ...

There is always a moment when the only response is the crackle of static and the only sound the hum of the aerial—except for the sharp breathing of anxious companions and the sound of your own heartbeat.

NINER, NOVEMBER GOLF OSCAR, THIS IS LORNA DOWNS STATION, RECEIVING YOU LOUD AND CLEAR ON TWO ZERO TWO ZERO. REPEATING . . .

Sighs of relief from all hands. We had been kindly lent a fifty watt Traegar transceiver and quickly learnt what a reliable unit it is in this country, but what with all the rolling round it took on the backs of camels, and being loaded on and off each day, we were always just that little bit relieved to hear 'loud and clear' from a station so far away.

That night I treated the team to an old camp recipe of 'bubbling slut'. The biltong is shaved into fine pieces, the mouldy outside of the bacon removed and the partially mouldy inside cut into small cubes, and these are boiled along with whatever dried fruit or vegetables come to hand, then garlic salt and a few beef cubes added. Meanwhile, rice is boiled in the other billy, drained and the meat broth tipped over the rice. The origin of the name, which I will not repeat, was once explained to me by a shearer's cook.

My back, which had been playing up for a few days now, kept me awake for a little while before the cosy glow of the fire and the familiar movement of the stars across the heavens lulled me to sleep. In the morning the pain had gone only to return with a vengeance later in the day. As we prepared to break camp we were spotted by three Land-Rovers full of tourists (or 'terrorists', as Paddy called them). They came over and delayed us by asking interminable questions and, to add insult to injury, insisted on posing with us and the camels while one of their camera buffs recorded the whole thing. When we finally did get away, they crossed our tracks after half a mile, and bipped their horns in loud farewell, which sent the camels scattering. We had begun to find that civilisation, when we encountered it, was an intrusion into our private lives; it was as if *they* had turned into aliens, not ourselves.

From the time of that incident, Frances did not settle down. She would lag back until her lead rope was strained, then break into a trot, forcing all behind her to follow suit, so that the team could not settle into an even pace and were tiring quickly. Worse, the number two camel's lead rope was tied to the back of the saddle on the number one camel (Ginger), which Paddy and myself rode in turn. When Frances pulled back, the gentle rhythm of the ride was broken with a sharp tug which jarred the whole body, and caused the rider's bottom to hit the saddle hard and the knees to chafe against the iron mid-hoop of the saddle. Both men and camels were getting short on tempers, and the air that morning was filled with language not heard there since the last bullock team passed through. In addition the heat was intense, and I was too burned from the day before to take my shirt off.

The country was still much the same, only now some stony ridges replaced the dunes to the west, the claypans still stretched to the eastern horizon. A movement up ahead under a stunted mulga bush caught Frankie's sharp eye, 'Marloo-Marloo!' They were far away and very alert, and when the Winchester kicked up dust some yards short, the big buck and two does bounded away to disappear across a stony scree to the north. Disappointed, we paused for lunch under the bush the 'roos had just vacated, and we could still smell the musky scent of the big buck. The jolting ride of the morning had rubbed a hole in the seam of one of the waterbags, so it was half a cup of water per man, and each person's swig was watched carefully by the other three.

Before proceeding, a nose-line was tied to Frances, which, after a few try-ons, calmed her down considerably. The mere knowledge that it was there did the trick, no longer did we have the 'lag and rush' progress of the morning's march. Although the heat was intense we made good miles, and were accompanied across the plain by a series of incredible 'willy-willies', which appear in the distance as tornadoes rising hundreds of feet in the air. There were numerous big clumps of dry saltbush here, and the 'willy-willies' picked these up and whirled them around at tremendous speeds before they got too high and dropped to earth again. One passed within a few yards of us, but only the slightest breeze could be felt from it and the camels took no notice at all.

A large rocky mountain rose out of the plain bearing east by north, and provoked an argument between Paddy and me as to our exact location. It was marked as PD (position doubtful) on our map, a comment we both tended to agree with. In mid-afternoon we crossed a flood plain two or three miles wide. There was tall Mitchell grass, lignum flats with a few red gum, cypress pine and leopard bushes scattered about, and inter-sected every hundred yards or so by narrow channels only a few yards wide and obviously drying up quickly. There was an odd, shallow mud pool in some channels surrounded by mud flats cracked by the heat like a shattered saucer, but the bird life clung on: the pigeons, finches, wag-tails and galahs rose noisily as we passed and the tracks of emus were visible beside a few of the stagnant wallows.

The map showed a homestead north-west of here, Breadalbane, where we hoped to buy a new waterbag, and, if possible, some sugar. After half an hour the windmill came in sight, but the trek across was pointless, the place was abandoned. Or almost abandoned; two dingoes shot out of the fallen-down chicken run as we approached. The door hung on one hinge and a loose roofing sheet creaked as it swung to and fro in the hot wind. No one. It had been well looked after once, a nice homestead, and some one had planted trees and shrubs to make a home of it. Without watering most were now withered stumps, but one tree clung on and was in full blossom. As we headed off dry and disappointed we passed a soli-tary grave set on the plain not far from the homestead, the paint blistered off the wooden headstone. Leaning at a slight angle, with the hot westerly whistling through the dead grass around it, the grave had an aura of incredible loneliness and desolation.

As we stood there a battered car came toward us along a bush track, leaving a trail of dust behind it, before clattering to a halt beside us. The driver was an elderly Englishwoman who had spent the last few years driving around the Australian back country on her own. She was a delightful character. Her equipment was spartan but functional and she asked us where the track led.

'Bedourie, about forty miles.'

'That will do nicely, thank you,' she replied.

As she had no sugar, nor we any petrol, we wished each other luck and went our separate ways. Paddy and I agreed that women like her made the British Empire what it was.

We trudged on and the countryside took on a familiar appearance with stony ridges, and to accompany it were the heat haze and mirages of Sturt's Stony Desert. As the camels were now moving well we kept going in order to put this country behind us, hoping to find water up ahead in a creekline clearly marked on the map, Thogomarra Creek.

At the end of nearly thirty miles we reached the creek at last light. It was a dry gully with a few sparse trees, but no water. We unloaded the camels in the creek bed and after a luke-warm cup of soup each we fell asleep on our swags, my back again reminding me of Burke and Wills. Dingoes howled to the west and south of us, perhaps the ones we had disturbed at Breadalbane. None of us really cared very much.

Dawn of the seventeenth of August was overcast, but the clouds cleared as the sun rose over the eastern plains. High stony ridges stood to the west, but the going was largely over the flat country alongside the Georgina 'River'. The ground was well covered with native clover and yellow cap, which gives the countryside a lush and attractive appearance as well as concealing the gilgais and large cracks in the dry soil into which we stumbled with monotonous regularity.

The Georgina 'River', in the dry season, is a flat plain about fifteen miles wide, rutted with numerous small creeklines, all dry, except for the occasional perennial waterhole. As Burke and Wills came through here, Wills noted that Camp 87 was almost exactly on the Tropic of Capricorn, on a creek with two or three small waterholes. The previous night they had camped on 'a fine creek two chains wide and fifteen feet deep', on a line running from north-east to south-west; this creek was three miles north-north-west of another waterhole two or three miles long.

Looking at the maps, and trying to fit into this scheme every waterhole in this latitude, it becomes evident that Camp 85 was on the Cuckoo Waterhole, Camp 86 on the Coorabulka Waterhole, and Camp 87 sixteen miles north and a little to the east of this, on 'a fine creek', which would have to have been what is now the Hamilton River, just to the north of the Tropic of Capricorn. It was obvious that they were slowing down across this flood plain, managing only five to fifteen miles a day. Perhaps the journey was starting to tell already, or perhaps they were giving the camels a bit of a break and feeding them up on the excellent browse.

With good reason, we were being very cautious of the browse on this plain, for a highly poisonous tree is supposed to grow here, *Acacia Georgina*, which has caused rapid deaths in stock hungry enough to eat it. Sure enough, soon we found it in abundance, growing on nearly all the creeklines, a twisted, distorted-looking tree with drab olive leaves, even the seed pods shrivelled and misshapen. To my horror, when I pointed it out to the others, Chilbi told me 'the camels bin eatin' 'em that fella las' night'.

We kept on, leaving Twelve Mile Mountain to the west and crossing the Tropic of Capricorn with no sense of elation, just glancing anxiously at the camels from time to time. They were fine, swinging along as if they knew, and were displaying their superiority over the lower beasts like sheep and cattle. They became quite partial to *Acacia Georgina*, and after a while we ceased to worry. The toxin is an unpredictable substance; sometimes this grotesque tree is quite safe stock fodder, at other times it causes horrendous losses, and the factors which determine the change are still a mystery.

As if to stress the fact that the Tropics start at the Tropic of Capricorn, it developed into a desperately hot day and the leaking waterbag meant short rations for all. Paddy trudged on in the lead, head down and whistling, the short water ration causing him to miss every second note, and the volume (thank God) being correspondingly lower.

To take my mind off water, I amused myself with the map, marking Burke's Camp 86 near the Five Mile Waterhole, and noting that the 'Five Mile' is ten miles from the 'Four Mile Hole' and that 'Twelve Mile Mountain' does not seem to be twelve miles from anywhere in particular. Looking at it, the 'Four Mile Hole' and the 'Five Mile Hole' are each the appropriate distance from the largest hole, the Coorabulka, where Burke had camped years before a homestead was ever built there. Twelve Mile Mountain is about fifteen miles south of Marion Downs homestead, but its rugged foothills start twelve miles from the station, thus the name.

This Australian habit of naming each creek according to its distance from one homestead can lead to the odd circumstance, when two homesteads are involved, of a traveller crossing the Four Mile, then the Nine Mile, the Six Mile then, some distance further on, the Five Mile. It can become confusing. I put the maps away, thought of water, and pulled out Wills' Diary to divert my mind from this fascinating topic.

In his notes for this leg, Wills, after mentioning that they camped on the Tropic line, remarked that he had taken some good latitudes at his last camp. Latitude observations are quick and easy, and give a traveller a good idea how far he is north or south of the Equator, or, in Burke and Wills' case, just how far they had to go to reach the Gulf. But Wills was not, apparently, taking star sightings for longitude, which would have told him how far east or west he was. Longitudes require much more time and take fairly complex mathematics to compute. I tried to picture Wills, exhausted at the end of a long day's march, trying to do the necessary calculations by firelight while the others slept, or asking Burke to pull the expedition up during the day while he worked it out. No, they had largely relied on their compass to point them north and only paused to take latitudes, their sole interest now being how far they had to go.

If that were so, they would have been heading about six degrees to the east of north, as compasses here are out by that margin, and over a thousand miles that error would push them fifty miles or more off course. This then, would explain why they arrived eventually at the Flinders River when they had hoped to reach the Albert River, a good way to the west. They had, of course, no way of knowing beforehand that the magnetic forces in this area would affect their compass.

All thirsty thoughts these, as for mile after mile we headed across numerous dry creekbeds. Ahead, on the other side of the flat, we could make out high downs country, and agreed that it would be good going, that anything would be good going after the ups and downs of the creekbeds. However, the downs proved to be some of the worst stone we had yet encountered, great sharp rocks the size of footballs. We would have been better off staying on the creekbeds.

The late afternoon sun picked out the roof of the Marion Downs homestead to the north, and we reached it, tired and thirsty, at sunset. The children of the homestead raced out to witness our strange cavalcade, and, in return for water and a jar of sugar, we gave them each a ride on a camel. The manager was away, but his wife was holding the fort, as wives have done since the pioneering days, and a woman's hand was obvious everywhere, with the flower beds and well-watered lawns. She was, as it turned out, an avid botanist, and was making a study of the wildflowers of the Channel Country. We left at twilight, waving goodbye to the children and promising to collect any unusual flowers for her. Alas, we never did.

Our camp was pitched beside a stagnant waterhole, and we brewed many a billy to make tea in which to dissolve our sugar. Then we boiled up again to give us drinkable water for next day. It may have been the children, or the homely atmosphere of the station, but something had touched a chord in me somewhere and I lay awake half the night thinking of my family and home. None of Burke's party had been married nor had a family, so none was torn between looking back and looking ahead.

I lay listening to the familiar night sounds, the frogs and crickets, the chirping of a small bat overhead, the crackle of the fire, the clink of the camel bell and the wind in the trees above us. Paddy always slept the sleep of the just, being able to finish his tea and be asleep before his cup was cold. Chilbi had a snore like an old cross-cut saw and he slept soundly, for a campfire to him was for many years all the home he needed. Frankie slept lightly, occasionally, in the midst of some bad dream, calling out in his own Arunda tongue before settling back to sleep. I shared his apprehensions and wondered what life lay ahead for this shy youth with the flashing grin, or, for that matter, what life offered for most of his people tomorrow. A dingo called far off as I too settled down, to dream of children playing blocks in front of a fireplace. We had come 500 miles from the 'Dig Tree' in twenty-seven days, and were three days behind Burke for our pains.

Next morning, dreams over, we saw signs of wild pig everywhere as we loaded up the camels. They are messy animals, fouling each waterhole they find and spreading such unsavoury diseases as tuberculosis and leptospirosis. But they have one saving grace: they are meat.

After the hard country of yesterday the morning was bliss, camels moving well across grassy flats well timbered with big, shady trees. We saw our first pig only five miles out from camp, a big black boar grazing on a river flat half a mile to the west. Paddy, the best shot among us, grabbed the rifle and ran bent double, down a shallow gully, keeping out of sight of the big boar and circling to get down wind of him. After a couple of hundred yards the gully ran out and Paddy was forced to stalk the pig through fairly open grassland, moving one slow step at a time, freezing whenever the boar looked up. We held our breaths in silence. I was trying to remember the smell of roast pork; Chilbi and Frankie were staring at their first wild pig. The boar by now was aware of something and his whole frame was tense and alert, snout sniffing the air and ears pricked. Paddy was just within firing range for the old Winchester, and was slowly raising the rifle to his shoulder.

Just then, tired of being held stationary, Ginger let out his mighty groaning bellow and the boar took off. Paddy managed to hit it a glancing blow but the pig disappeared into a ravine thick with tangled lignum bush. As Paddy raced in after him we could hear the sounds of other pigs moving excitedly down the ravine, but shortly after we saw our breadwinner re-emerge scratched, hot and empty-handed. With only a moderate curse or three for Ginger, he took the lead rope and headed off again, leaving the timbered channel flats behind and moving across a soft loamy plain. In the distant timberline to the west we could make out a herd of pigs grazing happily, but we marched on with disdain, for we could spare no time for long hunts.

It dawned on me that this was primarily the reason why Burke and Wills did not live off the land more. Any animals within a couple of hundred yards of a camel train are most certainly aware of its presence and thus very hard to approach, and to leave the train and walk half a mile, stalk for fifteen minutes and walk back empty-handed is a great time-waster as the team takes a fair while to fall back into rhythm. Thus to be on a tight schedule on a camel train is to eat poorly unless one camel is trained to leave the others and go out scouting, a very special camel indeed as generally they leave the group with the greatest reluctance. On this day, however, we were in luck, for late that morning a red doe broke cover from a thorn bush only fifty yards away, and Paddy dispatched her with one shot from the saddle. Marloo again! She was in excellent condition with no young in her pouch, a prize for any tuckerbag.

Chilbi prepared it in the time-honoured tradition, in this case quickly removing both hind haunches and tail. This is usually done, he told me, when the hunter is too far away to carry back the whole carcass, or when there are only a few mouths to feed. Otherwise the entire carcass is brought back. The haunch and tail, of course, represent only about half the weight of the carcass, but contain over eighty-five per cent of the meat on the 'roo, and almost all the body fat, so it seemed a sensible manoeuvre. Why carry double the weight back to get the last fifteen per cent morsel of food?

Happy now, we moved on past a 'dingo-proof' fence with dingo tracks on both sides and going right through it, until we met a man trying valiantly to muster up some scrub cattle in his utility only to send half of them bolting through a fence, and wrecking his gearbox in the process. There was a good camp near a waterhole up about ten miles, he said, we couldn't miss it, big tall trees all along it.

We pushed on again for another ten miles, but found no tall timber. By now the light was fading, so we made for a group of saplings where Frankie had seen corellas heading at drinking time. As we topped a gentle rise above this muddy soak, a herd of startled pigs scattered squealing in all directions, one of them falling to beady-eyed Paddy and the faithful Winchester. None of the others knew how to butcher a pig, or to check it for the various worms and diseases pigs carry, so the task was left to me. While Frankie got the fire going Paddy and Chilbi unloaded the camels; then Chilbi came over to view my handwork. He asked me why I opened up the belly and I explained that it was to check for signs of disease. To illustrate, I pointed out the kidneys, both of which I had discarded since they were full of worms, and tried to explain about checking a beast's organs for signs of tuberculosis, but his interest waned.

Suddenly I realised that our two systems of meat harvesting again represent the evolution of two different cultures. Our forefathers in the northern hemisphere harvested cattle and pigs, both carriers of tuberculosis and other potential dangers for man. The meat often had to be stored for a long time, so it was bled out and meticulously guarded against any bacteria which could build up over this time. Chilbi's system evolved in Australia where tuberculosis and these other diseases did not exist, and where the main danger lay in attracting too many flies by opening up the abdomen. It could never be stored here anyway.

Unfortunately, there was not enough water in the soak to wash the blood from my hands and arms, and while the pigmeat smelled delicious cooking in the coals, it did not taste so good with the smell of warm blood all over me, and the million or so flies that were attracted to it. As well, the soak provided no drinking water, and a thirsty night we spent. In the last rays of the sun we saw a pair of top-knot pigeons come in to drink but seeing us they swerved off with that strange 'trilling' noise of theirs. The corellas, which had been wheeling and screeching in droves overhead, finally settled down, to have their place in the sky taken by thousands of small bats. Later, an enormous feral cat came snooping around the carcass of the pig, his eyes glowing like coals in the firelight.

I lay back on my swag with a belly full of meat and a final cigarette noticing the fact that Chilbi would not eat pig, while Frankie happily gulped one piece after another in between bits of 'roo. Chilbi obviously now regarded this new food source, pig, with much the same enthusiasm as a member of the Melbourne Club would view goanna, even though he had happily eaten our salted bacon until now.

We got away early next morning, and had covered three miles before we came to the waterhole we had been told about. This was a pretty consistent finding on our trip: people in the age of motorised transport have lost all sense of distance. After all, a hole ten miles away takes them twenty minutes to reach, one thirteen miles away takes only six minutes extra. But on camel, that extra hour's walk can mean the difference between reaching the water before sunset or not, and motorists cannot appreciate the magnitude of the difference. After a while it became a game, to ask a person how far off such-and-such was, and then see how far it actually was. Most people could not tell within ten miles how far they had driven that day, but stockmen or drovers were generally correct to within half an inch or so of the nearest waterhole.

From this waterhole north the country started to change dramatically. We were now passing through thick black wattle scrub, some of which was in full golden blossom, and here for the first time we saw the mistletoe bird fluttering from one wattle spray to another. This beautiful bird is the size of a finch, his plumage a gleaming blue-black with a bright scarlet chest and sickle-shaped beak. The creekbeds and river flats were marked by huge ghost gums rather than coolibah, and kingfishers and rainbow birds flew between them as we passed, all sure signs that we were reaching more tropical latitudes.

Fences were becoming more and more numerous, indicating a closely settled region, and we tried to save time by following a track to Boulia. Our timing was bad for we were forced off the road seven times in two hours by a convoy of gigantic road trains, each consisting of a semi-trailer with an extra two trailers in tow. Their dust, and the fact that we had to get off the road and halt while they went past made for miserable progress. As well, my clean nylon socks put on especially because we were approaching a town, were not thick enough to fit the boots snugly, and for the first time on the trip I experienced really painful blisters.

We paused about 11.00 am to share the last of our water, about a mouthful each, and headed off again munching on a piece of pork and a piece of 'roo each, as by now Boulia was only a few hours' march away, and there we were to have a rest day. It is amazing how interminably long and tiring those last few miles before a rest can be, but by mid-afternoon, we had finally limped into our next camp-site. We set camp on the south bank of the Burke River, in what is regarded by local tradition as Burke's camp-site on January 8 or 9, 1861.

Above: **An early morning billy at Cordillo**

Overleaf: **The gibbers of the Stony Desert**

Following: Native **by Ludwig Becker**

14ᶜ
186

Across the river, and only a few hundred yards away, stood the little township of Boulia, Paddy's Mecca, for he had it on good authority that they sold chocolate here. After the camels were unloaded and hobbled, the gear stowed and swags unrolled, we set out for the town. Sure enough, it had a cafe which offered not only chocolate but also milkshakes and ready-to-smoke cigarettes known as a 'tailor-made' in these parts.

Our joy knew no bounds, and I sat reflecting over a vanilla milkshake and a 'tailor-made' that it would be an iron man indeed who could stop his men, or himself for that matter, from taking advantage of the trappings of civilisation when they were so close at hand. Of course, this meant that we were deviating from the food sources which had been available to Burke and Wills, thus rendering the whole experiment so much less meaningful. I accepted my weakness and drowned my disappointment in a cup of apricot-flavoured yoghurt, watching Frankie demolish a second chocolate milkshake. After all, Burke and Wills accepted fish and nardoo from the locals.

We collected the little mail which had made its way through a mail strike, and repaired to camp for an afternoon nap. Paddy swallowed the last of his chocolate in a gulp, pulled his hat over his eyes and was asleep. I took my boots off and brushed away enough grime to examine the blisters. Seeing they weren't too bad I turned to my mail.

The first item was a postcard from an aunt in Copenhagen, with a picture of the Little Mermaid in the bustling harbour. I felt she would have looked even more tranquil here beside the waterhole south of Boulia. The second item was a letter from an unusual friend of mine who had trekked alone through the remotest areas of south-west Tasmania on foot. He bid me good going, and remarked '. . . the first part of any journey is the simplest, relying only on physical strength. The next few hundred miles need determination.' How right he was. In lighter vein, he had included the centrefold of the previous month's *Playboy* magazine, 'to keep us company over the mountains'.

In reply, I sent a radio-telegram, which had to be coded so as not to offend delicate ears which listen to everything on the air.

Grateful for US survey map stop general outlines appear extremely favourable stop however details vague stop please send latest edition stop if that not possible send us original ore bodies for analysis stop. NOVEMBER GOLF OSCAR

He had, I heard later, spent a long time pondering that telegram before he deciphered it.

We had a good cook-up that night of all the left-overs from the fortnightly ration pack, finishing off with salami and cheese. Unfortunately, what with the loading and unloading each night, and camels standing on them occasionally, the rations were getting a bit knocked about, and towards the bottom of the pack we generally had a nutritious soup of condensed milk, sugar, matches, rice, flour and dried dates. Scraped off the inside of the leather pack and slapped on a piece of damper it tasted really dreadful.

That night we wended our way up to the hotel for a few quiet beers and were soon asked to a party by a group of local Aboriginals. Paddy and Frankie decided to turn in early, so Chilbi and I set off in the dark trying to follow the vague directions we had been given. On the way, we were talking about the stars and navigation, and I asked Chilbi about his people, and how they used to navigate. It was difficult for him to explain, but he said they never used the stars, simply 'They look all around them'.

I thought I knew what he meant. When I was a boy I knew that if I rode over to the big hill with one tree, followed the river down until it passed through some blackberry bushes and turned towards the three boulders, I would find a deep pond with fish in it. Was it like that, just knowing the country and keeping an eye on which way and how far you had come? A bit like that, Chilbi agreed, there's always tracks, signs, marks. I nodded, thinking to myself that his idea of tracks and marks was like our idea of stars; they are there if you know which ones to look for. But they certainly had no navigational use for the pointers or any other stars.

When I came to think about this later the obvious significance came to me. Even with a modern sextant and computer, I could not pinpoint my position to within a square mile. Had we, back in the Stony Desert, missed the soak at Bloodwood by fifty yards we could have perished. So, for a limited area, say a tribal territory in the desert, our system is useless; theirs is functional. Ours, of course, excels where vast distances are involved, especially where there are no landmarks and the target is large, say a sea voyage where one is heading for an island ten miles wide.

The talk of navigation closed as we came into a clearing where the Boulia Aboriginals were holding their moonlight party beneath a big kurrajong tree. Beer and flagon wine had replaced the Pitchery of Burke and Wills' time, but the hospitality was exactly the same, Chilbi being treated with a great deal of respect and courtesy because of his age and bearing. The party raged well into the night before the singing started, but the old tunes had gone, replaced by 'Slim Dusty favourites', and 'The Pub With No Beer'.

The next day passed rapidly, a 'rest' day with each man tending his chores, Paddy sweating profusely as he tried welding up one of the water tanks which was leaking worse than before.

We set out the following morning across a grassy plain, running parallel with the Burke River, determined to get the miles behind us before the day got too hot. The water tank which Paddy had tried to repair was leaking very badly and was almost totally useless.

Not long after Paddy took over the lead walk from me, a utility overtook us and the driver, Bob, owner of the cafe at Boulia, asked if I could come back to town to treat his dog which had been run over. I hushed Cleo down and quicky unhooked the medical bag, but it was to be of little use just when we needed it for inside everything was a dreadful mess. Bottles of disinfectants, anaesthetics, antibiotics and anti-emetics were shattered, tubes of anti-histamines and tropical lotions had squashed and bottles of tablets had popped open; the bag was coated with a foul gelatinous glue which could cure any known disease if only someone knew how to use it. I located a few surgical instruments and wiped them, salvaged some camel anaesthetic and headed back to town.

The dog was in shock and one hind leg shattered beyond repair; it had to be amputated. A table in the cafe was scrubbed clean, and Sister Wendy from the hospital helped with some human anaesthetic and suture material, but half way through the operation I realised it was not enough. As well as the leg injury the dog had a shattered pelvis, no chance of repairing that on a cafe table with hamburgers grilling a few yards away. I asked for a rifle to destroy the poor beast, and was given a light Russian rifle which I fired at her skull point blank; it was just powerful enough to penetrate the skin and awaken the dog from its half anaesthetised state into one of bewildered agony. Five shots it took; an experience I hope never to repeat as long as I live. Bob, who was obviously upset by the operation, had left us to it and had meanwhile occupied himself looking for something to replace our leaky water tank. He managed to locate two old cameleers' water drums on a nearby station. They had probably lain there for fifty years, but still held water. He offered them to us to help us out of our water problems. While we were testing the tanks our old friend Joe Scherschel from the American National Geographic Society turned up and offered to drive me out to the team, so we headed off and caught up with them about fifteen miles out. Somewhat subdued I thanked Joe for the ride and took hold of the lead rope. No-one asked how the operation went, they were all pretty hot and tired, especially Paddy who had to do all the walking, and it was probably obvious from my manner that things had not gone well. We pushed on hoping to make the 'Five Mile Lagoon' by nightfall, but darkness overtook us, so we camped on a claypan instead.

Frankie had shot a kangaroo while I was in town, so we prepared our evening meal. The inner thigh muscles (the adductors) are taken first and grilled in the coals, the stronger and more sinewy muscles are cut into slabs and thrown in the billy with salt and dried onions, and Chilbi does his specialty of the chef, the tail. It is thrown in the fire, skin, fur and all, and left there until the hair is fairly well singed. It is then pulled out to cool off, at which time it is scraped with a knife to remove the remaining singed hairs. Then a shallow trench is dug and filled with warm coals, the tail placed in it, and covered with more coals. Too hot and it burns; too cool, it is ghastly and greasy. But cooked 'just so', as Chilbi does it, it is a delight, tasting like a rather gamy ox-tail. For the connoisseur, the skin should be removed before eating, and on a poor specimen the last six inches of tail are not worth bothering with, but dogs love both tail and skin.

Not far from us were camped a couple of journalists who had driven down from Mt Isa for an interview. We did not (sour grapes) want to smell their sweet and sour pork cooking, and they did most certainly not want to smell our marloo, so the separate camps suited both parties. We could see their fire through the trees; an immense blaze in comparison with our meagre 'black-man's fire'.

Any bushman worth his salt can pick the difference between the remains of white man's and black man's fire by the fact that the latter is composed of a small pile of well-burned sticks, the former by several half-burned logs. Most whites will explain this by saying that 'the gins are too bloody lazy to collect any more than they have to'. In a way this is true, but not quite as simply as it is meant. Most white campers will pull up at a waterhole, four or five people, have a fire that night and depart for good the next morning, leaving their tins and bottles as souvenirs. Thus they have no need to conserve wood. but the tribes of fifteen to fifty Aboriginals needed a number of fires each night. At times tribes were camped on the one waterhole for three or four months, and if they had lit 'white man's fires' they would have cleared out all the useful wood for miles around. It is interesting that a white woman will happily burn two weeks' supply of wood in one night's camping, but at home turns her stove off as soon as a meal is cooked so as not to waste gas.

Another reason for small campfires was pointed out to me once by a doctor working on an Aboriginal mission. Since the fires are, by necessity, open fires and the centre of the social group, there is a tremendous incidence of body burns in children under two years of age who have toddled or crawled into the fire. A white man's fire would constitute an enormously greater risk of more serious burns.

The thought of burns reminded me suddenly that I had one last piece of 'roo cooking in the coals; it was difficult to distinguish from the other coals until we broke it open and knocked the burnt outside off. Frankie and I had half each, then turned in.

I had a dreadful night, trying to devise humane ways of putting down a dog which wouldn't die. Restless and half asleep, I heard the clink of camel hobbles beside me and for some reason knew that Larrikin, like the dog, had returned from the dead to reproach me. I sat bolt upright, only to find gentle Cleo standing a yard or so away chewing the cud, silhouetted against the moonlight. Reassured I lay back again comfortable on the soft clay, and slept soundly.

Dawn of the twenty-second saw us on the march across a flat Mitchell grass plain interspersed with low patches of scrub. 'Roo and emu were plentiful but very, very wary, seen only as fleeting objects in the distance. Occasionally, if one seemed to be moving a little more slowly, or had pulled up to hide behind a patch of myall or black wattle, one of us would head off, crouched in a run, to try and close on it. We had no success at all; once aware of the presence of the camels the game was on hair-trigger alert, and we were so low on ammunition we would not waste any on long-distance shots or moving targets.

There were probably a lot fewer, but more naive, targets on this plain when Burke and Wills passed, for the limiting factor in the red kangaroo populations is water, or more precisely, permanent water in drought years. They must drink water every four days or so during summer in these parts, which means they can only venture two days or so away from a permanent waterhole. In drought years that two-day diameter was soon eaten out and the population crashed if the drought was prolonged; at first the does simply failed to conceive, then pouch joeys died, later adults started to die.

When the white man came here he certainly caused some hardship for the red kangaroo with his guns and dogs, and his rabbits, cattle and horses eating the feed, but these were more than offset by the wells and bores he sank, providing permanent water. Oddly, this had a detrimental effect on the Aboriginals, who relied heavily on the accumulation of wildlife around waterholes in dry years but now found it dispersed to bores too brackish for man to drink. There are a lot of well-meant words spoken about the 'endangered' red kangaroo, but this only distracts attention from the animals really needing protection: the little numbats, rock wallabies, betongs and bandicoots.

We plodded across many small, dry creekbeds on the plain, all of which in this region are lined with negurra burr and Mexican poppy, both noxious weeds. The burr was especially annoying to us as it works its way inside socks and trousers, and, even worse, under saddles where it wears sores very quickly. In addition to the negurra burr and the Mexican poppy, the creeks we crossed had a third poisonous plant growing along their banks, *Acacia georgina* again, this time in great abundance.

As for the camels, Frances' pack sore was not healing as well as we had hoped. What she really needed was a spell from carrying a pack, a spell long enough to enable scar tissue to form. Still, she kept up the pace and had not lost much condition at all compared to some of the others.

We lunched beside a waterhole on Wills Creek, which the original expedition had crossed on January 10, 1861. The flies were very bad, coating our boiled kangaroo meat in a seething opalescent mass, which Paddy christendd 'roo garni'. In fact he had a colourful saying for just about every aspect of our humdrum lives. While others might go to the waterhole 'for a drink of water', Paddy would go to 'rinse his guts out'. We were to rinse our guts out properly that night, for late in the afternoon we passed Twin Rivers homestead, the home of Jack and Josephine Clarence, who invited us for dinner. We pushed on for another hour before setting camp on a creekbed, and returned to the homestead in our none-too-splendid 'best gear'. Our hosts treated us with typical country hospitality and the food was a vast improvement on 'roo garni'.

Tired and well-fed we trooped back to our camp, which took an hour to find, as the dying embers of the campfire were hidden by the high creek banks. It was a memorable farewell to the channel country.

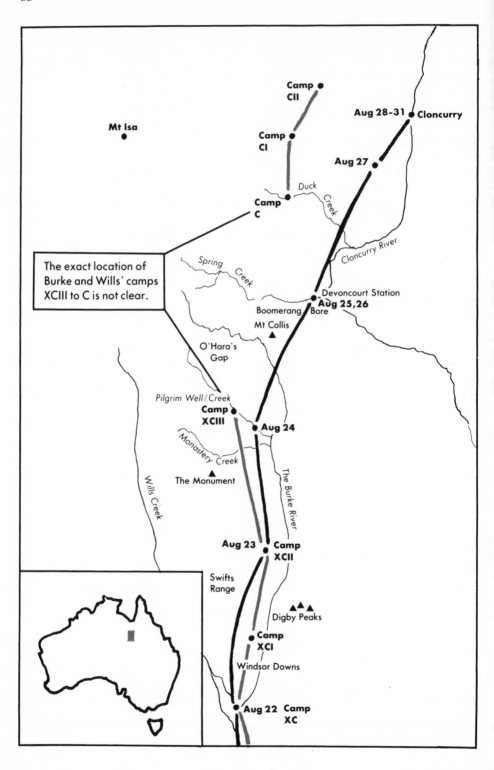

The exact location of Burke and Wills' camps XCIII to C is not clear.

THE LAND OF
THE KALKADOONS

Oh, heed my words of warning, mate,
don't hit your swag too soon,
nor close your eyes before sunrise,
in the land of the Kalkadoon.

Our route north took us past the Crimshaws' station, Windsor Park, where we spent a delightful hour yarning over a cup of tea before pushing on. The breeze blew from the south-west, moving the Mitchell grass gently around us and keeping the flies away. It was a beautiful day, the sky cloudless and the air crystal clear, while a vast rolling plain of Mitchell grass stretched ahead of us, with blue mountain ranges looming far off to the north and west.

As we marched across the plain I noticed that my shadow no longer had a belly on it , and on closer inspection neither did I. I was so absorbed in examining my newly visible ribs that I almost trod on a grass snake, one of many we saw that morning. The tracks of others were everywhere on the plain and they were obviously faring well on the quail, lizards and native mice which were abundant in the long grass. A pair of falcons circled overhead, keeping an eye open for small animals disturbed by our passage.

We had finally faced the truth that morning that our pork was no longer 'slightly off': it was rancid, and we jettisoned the putrid green slabs to lighten the loads. We halted for lunch on a rise, stone ranges now visible clear ahead. The breeze had dropped and the sun burnt down on the open plain as we squatted down to finish the last of the roo garni. It tasted a tiny bit off, but we had worked up an appetite so it was still 'kurra marra' (good meat). The brief meal over, we stood up and brushed the dust off, stuck the hats back on, and turned to face the ranges. We were not too worried as an old 'roo shooter had told us there was a track through them. There may have been in his time (he was over eighty) but there was no sign of one now, and it was the cruellest ground I have ever dragged an animal over. The ranges were sandstone, broken sharp stone rising to a ridge every half mile, then dropping abruptly into a gully again. The camels strained up the loose shingle on the climbs and slipped and slid down each gully. Every so often we had to cross limestone outcrops, some as smooth as a marble floor, others broken into sharp piles of rubble. As well, this was our first taste of 'mountain' spinifex, a large bushy plant with long spikes which penetrate trousers and skin, leaving our legs covered in itchy sores. Our faces and arms were suffering as well, striped in welts from the thick acacia scrub. It seemed that it would never end, mile after mile of climbing, falling, spinifex, limestone, acacia and flies.

Exhausted, we stopped and called a half-hour break to spell the camels. We were on a limestone ridge with a view to the south and east. It has been said that this whole mass of ranges which now lay before us was once a gigantic island, some 20 000 square miles in extent, set in an ancient fresh-water sea. Thus the limestone on which we now stood was part of a fossilised 'barrier reef'. A few yards away from us lay an unusual formation of stone. We pottered over out of curiosity to find the entrance to an enormous cave, the mouth of which was about fifteen feet in diameter. The cave itself went straight down into the range, a vertical drop of at least sixty feet, as near as we could judge by the sound of falling stones. The entrance lay in such a position that it would have to catch a lot of the run-off from the ridge, thus the cave had probably been carved out by water. But where did the water go then? We reckoned that that cave must either go for miles and empty out on the plain, or else contain within it an enormous reservoir which gradually seeps away.

Nearby an echidna's tracks meandered off to the right, and as I followed them wondering idly what echidnas taste like, I noticed three stone spires across a valley to the east, lit up by the afternoon sun. The three cones! As they made their weary way back from the gulf, Wills had written:

Wednesday, 20 March, 1861—Camp 32R ... had to camp for the night. At the junction of the two creeks just above are the three cones, which are three remarkably small hills to the eastward.

This was a tremendous find as a number of historians have believed that the return journey was made a hundred or so miles east of here. Yet there they stood, a geological feature so unique that there could no longer be any doubt as to the return route. While blazes on trees can be forged or obliterated the three rocks cannot; they stand as eternal monuments.

And it was to be within one hour's toil over more broken ranges that we made our second discovery. As we looked ahead to the north we saw that we were almost over this small range. But we saw more than that. Wills wrote in his diary:

Saturday, 12 January, 1861: We then entered a series of slaty, low, sandstone ranges ... the more stony portions are, however, covered in porcupine grass, and here and there with mallee ... from the highest portion, which we reached at a distance of about seven

miles, we had a pretty good view of the country towards the north. As far as we could see in the distance, and bearing due north, was a large range ... The east end of this range just comes to magnetic north. On the west of this, and bearing NNW, is a single conical peak, the top of which only is visible ... From here a descent of two miles brought us to a creek ...

And there it all was, laid out before us, just as Wills had described it, 'the brothers' and 'O'Hara's Gap' to the north, appearing as a solid range, 'the Monument', a solitary sandstone spike bearing nearly north by north-west (Wills was not aware of compass error in this region, and so his compass bearings are about six degrees out). Below us, about two miles off, was the creek on which he camped.

My calculations showed that they had passed only a couple of hundred yards to the west of where we now stood. By working back from this point using Wills' diary and the few cryptic comments left by Burke and King, we could, as a result of today's discoveries, reconstruct their progress in this region both going up and returning. Until now this had been a matter of guesswork.

Our elation was dampened by the fact that both Paddy and I had been, for the last few hours, suffering from the most dreadful stomach cramps and diarrhoea, the probable result of 'roo garni. We made for the creek below as quickly as our exhausted camels could travel, unpacked and searched through the ruins of the medical kit for a suitable cure, which thank God we found intact. Reduced now to biltong and dried peas for the main course we ate greedily, and to celebrate the day's discoveries I opened one of our six tins of peaches in syrup, which we divided between us like four hungry dogs, despite the stomach cramps.

Wills remarked of his camp on this creek that 'we found here numerous indications of blacks having been here, but saw nothing of them'. They may have seen nothing of the Aboriginals, but the latter were following their progress very carefully indeed. King reports that 'when we came in sight of ranges ahead we saw several volumes of smoke to the east and west'. These were not wisps from tiny cooking fires, they were the signal fires of the Kalkadoons. Without being aware of it, Burke and Wills had just entered the territory of Australia's most dreaded tribe of mountain warriors and were trespassing where no plains Aboriginal would dare set foot. The progress of the first white men ever to come here was being followed closely.

The Kalkadoons were a mountain race of outstanding physical appearance, many over six feet tall, and were an exceedingly proud and warlike people. They resisted the take-over of their land longer than any other tribe, using guerilla warfare and taking advantage of the rugged features of their domain. Indeed, they may well have held their territory indefinitely had it not been discovered in the 1870s that their mountains were rich in gold, silver and copper as well as other minerals. From then on the rush of eager prospectors and, later, settlers led to a series of

increasingly bloody encounters between the whites and the various
Kalkadoon clans. The Queensland Government then decided to pacify
the region using mounted police recruited from coastal tribes and
appointed, as officer in charge, Marcus de la Poer Beresford, who happened to be the cousin of Lord Charles Beresford. The reaction of the
Kalkadoons to this intrusion was swift and brutal, as recorded in
Queensland Police archives: 'On January 24, 1883, Inspector Marcus de
la Poer Beresford . . . and his troop of native mounted police, were trapped in a mountain gorge and massacred by Kalkadoons.'

Following this outrage against civilised behaviour in general (and the
British aristocracy in particular), more troopers were sent in under the
command of the sub-inspector of police, F C Urquhart, to crush the
troublemakers. The Kalkadoons, however, having now tasted victory,
became bolder in their attacks and 'as the forces sent against them
increased more and more, joined together to ward off the invaders. In
September of 1884 they made a fatal mistake: massing the warriors of
many clans at Prospectors Creek and abandoning their guerilla tactics,
they formed ranks and marched towards the waiting Snider carbines of
Urquhart's entrenched men. Time and again they were forced back but
each time they re-grouped their thinning ranks, and again marched forward until they fell. It has been estimated that hundreds of warriors died
in that battle, which must surely rank with the 'Charge of the Light
Brigade' as one of the most heroic gestures of defiance in human history.
It seems strange that this battle, perhaps the biggest ever to take place
on Australian soil, is not mentioned in school history books. Today, a few
integrated Aboriginals still boast of the Kalkadoon blood, but their power
is a thing of history.

Our course next day was determined for us, as it had been for Burke
and Wills. Ranges closed in to the west and east, and there was a wide
grassy plain to the north, so we packed up the camels, uttered our early
morning 'let's hit the road again' war cry at which the camels would lurch
to their feet in that back-and-forward manner, and headed due north. The
camels moved very slowly that day. The bumping and bruising by packsaddles as we crossed the range had aggravated old packsores and started
new ones. Flies attracted to the weeping sores for moisture caused them
to become infected, and a camel's woolly fleece is an ideal habitat for
maggots to grow. We were in trouble, for 'fly-strike' was the last problem
I had expected, and with our limited medical kit we were almost
powerless to deal with it. The problem vexed me as we trudged north.

Up ahead, about half a mile off our path, the sails of a bore were visible,
so I suggested that we pull up and fill the water tanks there. Paddy argued
that the mile there and back was not worth it, we would get water later
in the day. We bickered for a mile or more on the matter, then agreed
that if there were cattle there, and thus water, we would cross and fill
up. There were cattle, so we filled up.

On any trek like this personal differences show up, magnified by the isolation. Paddy and I were very different but both fairly determined so we argued over the minor things that were made to seem so important in our long dreary day's march. On occasions we seemed subsconsciously to seek arguments simply to give our minds something to do.

'How far to Pilgrim Well?'

'About sixteen miles.'

'I make it nearer seventeen.' (Pause while map and ruler come out.)

'Sixteen point four miles.'

'Was nearer seventeen when I asked.'

'Bull!'

As well, our basic approach to problems was different. I have always tended to sit back and weigh up all the factors I can think of before deciding anything, thus at times missing opportunities when they arise. Paddy seemed to me to leap in and do things without bothering to consider the risks, so at times each made errors which riled the other. But we found that such differences are essential in any team, for we faced many problems requiring different approaches. While I could prod and poke at a camel and eventually figure out what his bellowing was about, Paddy must first fight the cranky brute to a standstill, throw him and hold him down while I did my prodding and deciding.

I reflected as I walked along that a similar relationship must have developed on the original expedition. Wills was a meticulous scientist and well organised, but he lacked any colour, any flair. He was not a leader. Burke, on the other hand, was hopelessly ignorant of navigation, rationing or organising his men, but he had the dash and charisma of a natural leader and men either loathed him or followed him to their deaths without ever questioning his leadership. Between them they held qualities that are rare today. We certainly couldn't pretend to have them; perhaps our era does not produce the type of man to whom success is more important than life itself.

The party must have been a little apprehensive, though, as they marched across this plain towards Pilgrim Creek, for the detail of the Selwyn Ranges is grimly visible here, ironstone skeletons of a pre-Cambrian range crumbling into jagged ridges. To the west the Standish Ranges, while blurred by distance, are even more menacing, growing higher and merging with the Selwyns on the northern horizon. The Kalkadoons, watching silently from their mountains, must have thought the expedition so tiny and frail as it wandered across the plain, heading due north to the mountain passes.

The plain consists of rolling Mitchell grass flats crossed by a number of dry creek-beds lined with spinifex and the flats are broken up by occasional mallee scrubs and low rocky outcrops. The creeks have colourful names which leave the traveller wondering about their origins. Prickly Bush Creek was obviously well named, and Dead Horse Gully is obvious, too, but what of Monastery Creek without a monastery, or, for that matter, what story lies behind the name of Petticoat Creek? They were all dry, and would not contain water until the wet season, in summer, and even then they merit their name 'creek' for only a few days at any one stretch.

In fact we struck no more water that day until sundown when we trudged into Pilgrim Well, a bore at the junction of Petticoat, Pilgrim and Yellow Waterhole Creeks and probably the site of Burke's Camp 93.

Situate at the junction of three sandy creeks in which there is an abundance of water. The sand is loose and the water permeates freely, so that the latter may be obtained delightfully cool and clear by sinking anywhere in the bed of the creeks.

This might have been so in 1861, but in 1977 the water tasted strongly of cow dung, even the bore water tasted better. The birds thought so too, thousands of galahs descending to drink at nightfall while cattle wandered over to our campfire and gazed at us as we chewed our tough biltong. We were meat hungry again and the thought of fresh steak was quite appealing, but it is not done to shoot and eat someone else's bullock without asking first. We tried to sing them as the dream-time medicine men are supposed to have done, calling them into the cooking pot. No law against that. 'Here, bullock-bullock. Here bullock-bullock.' No response. No steak. Back to biltong.

While Burke was camped here the scene back at Menindee was one of bustling activity, for money had been sent up from Melbourne, and now the newly purchased pack horses were being broken in. Wright's time was divided between breaking in horses and sorting through the fifteen odd tons of stores which Burke had left, trying to decide which items would be needed on the trip to relieve the depot up at Cooper's Creek. This was a vitally important task, as even with the extra horses only two tons could be carried. The rest of the team were busy killing bullocks and drying out the meat, sewing pack bags out of old sacks and fitting them onto the new packsaddles. It was the height of summer at Menindee and the midday temperatures soared over one hundred degrees, drying out the country between them and Cooper's Creek where they would soon be heading.

Up on the creek the four men at the depot were isolated from the rest of the world and had had no word from Burke in the north or from Wright's party, which they had expected for over a month now. Brahé was obviously on edge to judge from his diary.

6 January 1861. A large number of natives came to the camp, whose demeanour roused my suspicions. Got hold of a young native and shoved him off, when he fell down. In the afternoon the whole tribe returned, the men armed, some with spears and some with boomerangs; most of them had painted their faces and bodies. I met them at a short distance from the camp, and marked a circle round it, I gave them to understand that they would be fired at if they entered it. On some of them crossing the line I fired off my gun into

the branches of a tree, then they retired and did not molest us any more.

Frankie was a bit upset when I retold the story over the waning fire, but I never determined whether he was upset by the behaviour of Brahé or the Aboriginals. It was a fine warm night as we turned in. We had covered 645 miles from the 'Dig Tree' in the last thirty-nine days, and despite the pace we were forcing on the poor camels, we were still a day behind Burke, with 300 miles yet to go.

Two options were open for the next day's journey. We could go due north from here and cross a saddle on the eastern end of Mt Collis, or we could go further east and cross the rise near O'Hara's Gap. Looking north from here the latter appears easier going, and after the rough ranges two days earlier even Burke would probably have chosen this course. King mentioned that they travelled over grassy plains at this time, so they very likely did come this way.

The country ahead was thick mallee for some miles, and then opened out onto Mitchell grass downs. The mallee had slowed down our progress a little, but once on the downs the camels strode out, and we had covered a mile or more before Chilbi's sharp eyes picked out something. We were travelling with six camels, so that Chilbi, on Alice at the rear of the column, had been watching the tracks of five camels for the last six hundred and fifty miles. But now he saw six sets. Checking the tracks of all of ours, we realised that we had crossed the tracks of an enormous wild bull camel. The tracks were fresh—two cigarettes old, Chilbi reckoned—or in our terms about half an hour.

Once or twice each year bull camels come into season or 'musth', a condition in which they become extremely aggressive, and such a beast had attacked four motorists in Saudi Arabia recently, killing three and nearly scalping the fourth. By his tracks, this one, at least as big as Wallaper, was moving about quite rapidly. We had only one bullet left for the Winchester, which we now carried loaded for the first time on the trip. We pushed on warily, spotting freshly browsed desert oak here and there which marked his progress. From the height of it he was a very big camel. Thank God we never met him.

Around morning break we came across another set of tracks, a cow and a new-born baby; her tracks were of similar size and spacing to Alice's while the baby's tracks were tiny by comparison and taking three steps to her one, not always in the same direction. We thought for a while of going after her, as breeding cows and calves both fetch good prices nowadays. But we had to push on and our camels by now were looking so poor it was doubtful if we could have run her down in any case. By lunchtime we were passing a number of rocky jump-ups and heading through fairly open country, and we started seeing Marloo, first one, then a few, then hundreds. As luck would have it our last bullet was wasted on the first one we saw, a moving target bounding diagonally across a jump-up. After that we saw them in droves, either moving off slowly as we approached or lying quietly on their sides beneath a scrawny acacia bush, quietly passing the heat of day. The thermometer showed over 40°C by lunchtime and for the first time the presence of moisture was noticeable in the air—it no longer had the ability to dry sweat instantly the way it did back in the Stony Desert. The air was still and heavy as we hushed down for lunch at O'Hara's Gap, a treasured piece of salami each, some dates and a couple of figs, which were covered in ants and tasted like formic acid. The salami was going off a bit too, but the dates were pleasant enough.

Lunch over we faced a broad sweeping slope covered in grass a metre high. It was scarred at irregular intervals with deep erosion gullies which had us detouring more than progressing. The long grass made a swishing noise as we filed through, and numerous small grass snakes slithered out of our way. They are apparently quite harmless, but where they occur in large numbers like this you generally find living off them the larger taipans and brown snakes, not so harmless. I wished the long grass would not make that swishing noise.

In any event we descended the slope unscathed and after two miles we entered a thick mallee scrub. The afternoon sun baked down on us as we pushed on plagued by black bush flies which were attracted by the sweat on our faces and the sores on Cleo, who had been off-loaded.

By mid-afternoon it was still hot and sticky when we encountered a rig team at Boomerang Bore, pumping the tank full as the windmill was useless without wind. 'Twelve miles to Devoncourt', we were told. A moment of congratulations for Paddy and me as we had both calculated our distance covered that day to the nearest hundred yards and were right on target.

The sandy soil over which we now travelled was marked more and more frequently with camel tracks and the acacia and casuarina scrub lining the winding creek beds had obviously been browsed in the last few weeks, but the camels managed to stay out of sight. At last, just on dusk we limped down onto Spring Creek, a tributary of the Cloncurry River, and followed it up until we hit a cool shallow pool shaded by tall trees.

The camels, once unsaddled, headed down to the creek to slurp up a couple of dozen gallons each before shuffling off to graze as fast as their hobbles would allow them, Cleo's hip showing white in the gathering darkness where the white paste coated her packsore. The night fell swiftly and became suddenly quite cold. We rolled out our swags and lay back around the fire watching the billy boil and the biltong stew bubble away. For a change we were to have rice with it.

Our old friend Joe Scherschel drove down from the homestead a few miles away (we had been in touch with him over the Flying Doctor Radio) and offered to drive us in to the pub for a beer before we turned in. We obliged him like a shot. It was a strange sensation to be in a car covering thirty miles an hour or more and I noticed that we all tended to hang on tightly. The pub was a small, weatherboard structure with a wide verandah badly in need of repair. A couple of old timers held up the far end of the bar, otherwise it was deserted. The barman lifted his head off the bar and eyed us suspiciously. 'What do you bloody want?' seemed to be his hospitable greeting to any thirsty travellers. 'A beer,' we said in unison, and he peered at us for a while as though we had replied in Urdu or Polish, then shuffled off slowly to find some beer. I suppose our appearance was a bit off-putting. Bluey coats pulled up around our ears, hair now long and matted and our faces streaked with the sweat and dust of the last few hundred miles. Come to think of it our smell was probably a bit off, too.

We were each handed a warm stubby of beer and the opener was pointed out to us, then the barman turned his back on us while he counted the change, coin by coin. Perhaps Paddy was right, perhaps this was 'the meanest little sod God ever shovelled guts into'. It was an enjoyable night apart from that, for a few more locals drifted in and we were soon sitting round yarning, and a miner pushed his tin hat back and sang an aria in Italian as we left.

Home in camp once more we stoked the campfire and put the billy on for a light night cuppa. We had done one hundred and twenty-six miles in the last five days, the camels were tiring, and Wallaper was stone-sore, so we decided to camp here a day.

We were rudely woken up as the dawn rang with the sounds of a herd of steers galloping past us to the waterhole. We had obviously camped too close to their drinking trail, and they had been mustering up the courage to pass us all night, too stupid to find another path.

Still tired, I stretched, scratched the head a bit and looked around for the camels, then realised it was a rest day and settled back into the swag for an extra hour's kip. As I pushed my way into the swag the smell of foetid socks and feet emerged from its depths but I dozed off anyway. Some time later I opened an eye and surveyed the scene. Chilbi had the fire going, its smoke was drifting up through the river gums, Frankie was ambling back from the creek with a billy for tea, and Paddy had his socks off and was prying his toes apart. Between us we had devised a technique to determine whether or not socks need washing: you peel them off and then fling them against a ghost gum; if they drop they are O.K., but if they stick to the tree you are due to wash them.

From Wills' diary it appears that the original team had few changes of clothing, and had probably felt just as grubby as we were. They would have felt our panic, therefore, when we heard that the State Governor and his wife had arrived at Devoncourt Station from Brisbane and were being driven over to meet us. None of our usual rest day routine today! The camp swung into a hive of activity, mess gear washed in the creek, best shirts on, swags rolled, cake of germicidal soap dredged up from the bottom of the veterinary bag (and actually used), socks pulled off the ghost gums.

I cannot honestly say that we presented a splendid sight when the viceregal cavalcade appeared, but it was the best we had looked for some time, and we had dragged up sufficient logs for a traditional white man's fire. As they shook hands with us I could distinctively smell their soap and I winced, hoping to God they could smell ours. I need not have worried for the visit was very friendly, and the Macdonalds from Devoncourt had brought some glasses and cold drinks so we did not have to take turns drinking black tea out of our chipped and stained enamel mugs as we had feared. In fact it was a relaxing afternoon as the Governor was an ex-navigator in the Navy and quite interested in the minutiae which we were investigating. In fact he offered some worthwhile bits of advice. There was no need to stoke the fire after they had gone, since it was still four or five times our usual size, very impressive in fact.

We were joined by Joe and two other journalists, John and Bob, for tea that night. These two had been looking for us for a couple of days and finally caught us on our test transmission. As they were twenty miles off course we radioed them in and in gratitude John, a trained cook, made a very passable 'roo-bourgignon' with a 'roo Paddy had taken on a borrowed bullet. Just then, too, Paddy's sister and brother-in-law drove up and joined our camp for the night. The clean clothes, the day's rest, the company and the bonfire all combined to give our camp a festive feeling and we sat around the fire yarning long after the moon was up. Over a cuppa we found out what was happening in the outside world. Elvis Presley had died, there had been a postal strike and Parramatta were odds-on for the minor premiership. Some people had 'phoned in to say they were interested in our trip, others thought we were just a bunch of ratbags.

And where, I was asked, were we going from here? I had to admit I was baffled. We had definitely been on Burke and Wills' track, or within half a mile of it, back at the Swifts Range, but from Pilgrim Well there were no entries in Wills' diary for five days. King mentions in his undated notes that after the slaty ranges they had passed over well-grassed, well-watered country for sixty miles until they came to a dead stop, 'nothing to be seen but ranges'. That would be about here somewhere. They had then apparently tried to cut through the ranges to the west but failed and returned east. Wills' next entry, on January 19, 1861, has them crossing the range at about this latitude but no one knew exactly where. Burke, in one of his brief notes, remarked the next day that he determined to go 'straight at the ranges'. It was quite confusing and left us with many options. When there is an easy way out, and other factors are equal, I can be as weak as the next man (or even show him a trick or two) so I chose to go north-north-west, then turn through the mountains via the well-worn Chinaman's Creek Pass, where the Duchess track runs. As we busied ourselves breaking camp at dawn we shared a certain sense of apprehension, however, for it was still not going to be any picnic. We led the camels down along the river bed as the sun rose over the craggy peaks of the Selwyns, striking the upper branches of the white gums above us.

Above: Coaxing the camels through high rocks

Overleaf: Breaking camp as the sun rises

Following: At the Gulf, Paddy and Frankie mark the last camp

The end of the journey for Tom and Paddy at Saltwater Creek on the Gulf of Carpentaria

It was such a beautiful morning, crisp and cool, with soft powdery soil underfoot that Paddy and I walked along together leading the camels and singing in harmony.

After a few miles winding through the riverine mallee flats, we passed Devoncourt homestead and said farewell to our hosts and our visitors of yesterday.

Already the heat of the sun could be felt and once off the river flats the ground started to become harder and more stony. The rises at first were almost imperceptible, nothing more than flinty downs country such as we had met before, but gradually the inclines became steeper, the gibbers larger, and Wallaper became more and more difficult to manage. The scattered tussocks of grass here were short and dry and the ranges around us were dotted with a few gnarled and stunted acacia bushes with the odd grass-trees starting to appear. If eaten, these cause a peculiar brain cell degeneration in cattle. After some time the beasts behave peculiarly, wobbling about on their hind legs like drunks. Yet another plant which I hoped our omnivorous camels would pass over.

We had come fifteen miles by lunchtime and as we crossed Duck Creek we saw a delightful waterhole to which we made our way along the bank, two blue cranes taking off as we did so. The banks of this creek, like so many others, were lined wih negurra burr but we managed to find a clear patch of earth beneath a river gum. Opposite us a tiny kingfisher perched on a dead limb, eyeing off the fish below him, the smallest of which was twice his size. His lunch, if he caught one, would be substantially better than ours.

We hit the road as soon as our lunch was swallowed and soon found ourselves climbing a steep ridge, entering a narrow pass between high mountains. By now Wallaper was nigh-on unmanageable, pulling back every ten paces. And when Wallaper pulled back the lead camel was brought to a jarring halt, the others shuffling along to a standstill. He had been stone-sore ever since we crossed the Swifts Range, and the gibber here was loose, and tumbled under his big pads, bruising them further. We made it over the ridge and began a long descent, and he was, if anything, worse. Below, a waterway cut across our path and though it was now dry we halted for a while to rest him, flopping down ourselves to share a quiet smoke.

The narrow pass through which we had just come widened here into a valley about half a mile across. The waterway continued down its length meandering along through open woodland, slender trees growing on the sketchy clay and shingle plain which was marked everywhere by termite mounds. These were brick red in colour and about two feet high, and since they all face the same direction they gave the upper reaches of the valley the appearance of a rusty graveyard. In between them were scattered tussocks of dry spear grass and spinifex.

The valley was surrounded by broken ranges, the remains of a once majestic range. The crumbling cores still stand like old mountain fortresses perched on the rubble slopes of their former grandeur, eroding away in the heat and wind. How could Burke, or anyone else, look ahead at these and calmly say, 'I determined today to go straight at the ranges . . .', when two days earlier he had written, 'Still on ranges, camels sweating profusely with fear'? But Burke first turned west and headed straight at the mountains there (and Aboriginals told that the Kalkadoons saw him forty miles to the west of his supposed crossing point), and then instead of searching for a mountain pass he headed straight across these ridges. Wills' diary indicates that in doing so he certainly surprised some Kalkadoons.

Saturday, 19th January, 1861—. . .On our being about to cross one of the branch creeks in the low range, we surprised some blacks—a man who, with a young fellow apparently his son, was upon a tree cutting out something; and a lubra with a piccaninny. The two former did not see me until I was nearly close to them, and they were dreadfully frightened; jumping down from the trees, they started off, shouting what sounded to us very like 'Joe, Joe'. Thus disturbed, the lubra, who was at some distance from them, just then caught sight of the camels and the remainder of the party as they came over the hill into the creek, and this tended to hasten their flight over the stones and porcupine grass.

I had entertained a vague hope that this creek, Chinaman's Creek, was the one down which Burke had come, but the further we advanced along it the less it fitted Wills' description since the alignment was wrong (for once fitting exactly to the course shown on our maps). Lower down the valley its appearance improved a little; the black trunks of ironbarks stood out among golden strands of wattle and the course of the creek was marked by white ghost gums. A tall shrub was in flower, large purple blooms growing off its spindly tangled stems, but these odd splashes of colour seemed out of place in this inhospitable part of the world.

It was late in the afternoon, when the valley was in the shadow of the western range and the sunlight lit up the peaks and spires to the east, that we were hit by locusts. At first the odd one, then a few more at decreasing intervals, then literally thousand upon thousand of them smacked into us, disturbed from feeding on the bushes we passed. Overhead they swirled in a silvery grey cloud which lasted for miles. We reached the end of it only shortly before camp.

The ground here was still stony, a poor camp site with little suitable camel feed and no water, but the camels had had enough work for one day. Wallaper had been a little better in the afternoon but not much, and both Cleo and Frances were tiring badly. That night, wriggle and dig as much as I might, I could not get comfortable for our swags were laid on a bed of gibber, and each one removed merely made the ground more uneven. Even Paddy slept badly, cursing Wallaper and Frances in his dreams. The camels stayed nearby, too knocked up to scout out the sparse vegetation available.

We were up stiff and sore before Orion faded in the dawn, and we saddled and left the spot without breakfast, without talking, without even a glance back to mark the site from the north. To us it was not worth remembering, which was unfortunate as we left our camel bell there somewhere.

The valley was still in deep misty shadow but the cliffs and spires above us were bathed in sunlight and the first heat of the day reflected down from them. The creek wound round and disappeared through a narrow cleft in the cliffs which I had originally hoped to be 'The Gap' mentioned by Wills, a spot he described as 'the most dangerous part of our journey'. Although man had altered the narrow pass by pushing a railway and road through, there is enough relatively undisturbed ground to see that this stretch in no way compared with some of the country they had crossed earlier. The cliffs rose high and sheer on each side and were pocked by fissures and caves, but the watercourse itself would have offered reasonable going for them. Chinaman's Creek was not the 'upper reaches of the Cloncurry' along which they had travelled. It was, however, the edge of the Kalkadoon lands, and we searched for any of the crane's foot paintings on the rock faces which they used to mark out their boundary. We saw none. Disappointed we pressed on, heading north-east up a wide valley, and again encountered the locusts in their millions. There was scant vegetation here to attract them, but what little there was they were demolishing at an incredible rate as though to justify their being chosen as one of the seven plagues of Egypt.

Although isolated low ranges still stood ahead to the west and north-east, the countryside now took on a much gentler appearance—more rolling rises and with soil covering their rock frames. Fence lines started to appear more frequently and soon after midday we were to strike for the bitumen road which runs from Cloncurry to Mt Isa. Some miles to the west of us the Cloncurry Shire Council had erected a stone cairn on this road with an inscription stating that Burke and Wills had passed through there on January 22, 1861, thus heading for the Corella River and not the Upper Cloncurry.

The heat was such that we ceased to care much either way, but forced ourselves and the camels to push on, to get this sticky, hot bitumen behind us. Cars hurtled past and honked their horns or pulled up in a screech of brakes and a cloud of dust, neither of which were welcomed. Alongside the road the white man had marked his domain by broken bottles, rusted cans and old newspaper, all presided over by a billboard showing four Swedish pop singers and a message to keep Australia beautiful.

Cleo had shown obvious signs of fatigue early on in the day, and had started to sweat profusely. We off-loaded her and thus had to walk all day. When one day is the same as the next, without a definite goal beyond a good day's march, the timeless atmosphere of the bush pervades everything and there is no rush. But this march on bitumen was dragging as we impatiently sought to reach Cloncurry, for here we were to rest up for a couple of days, with our families who were flying up to meet us. It was galling to see the cars fly by or stop to tell us we were only nine or ten miles out; three hours' hard march for us but only ten minutes or one can time for them.

At long last we trudged into town from the west and crossed the Cloncurry River, down which we were now convinced we should have come. A fair number of townspeople had come out to greet us and the Shire Council had kindly made arrangements for the camels to be kept on a recreation reserve for the couple of days.

We pulled up beside the first shop we saw and went in for a cold lemonade and some tailor-made cigarettes and, of course, some chocolate for Paddy. We were about to sit and enjoy ourselves when we heard a commotion outside, where our camels knelt resting on the roadside surrounded by goggle-eyed children. A very drunken stockman had decided to have a ride on Ginger who was bellowing his disapproval and looked just about ready to bolt, straight through the surrounding children. Following a brief but heated discussion on the stupidity of taking someone else's camel for a ride, we headed off through town for the reserve, where we wearily began to unload. At that moment my wife and parents drove up, and all thoughts of Burke and Wills vanished in the happiness of reunion, cries of 'I hardly recognised you, you're so thin' and 'God, you're filthy' offsetting the more endearing remarks.

That night was like a fairytale, sitting round in a modern motel sipping champagne, smelling of soap and feeling the crisp sensation of a clean and ironed shirt, not to mention the company of my family who seemed at first to belong to another life, so remote did it appear now. When I was combing my hair it had taken me a time to re-accustom myself to the image in the mirror, my hand moving in what appeared to be the wrong way and the bed that night, though soft and clean, was just too yielding and insecure for sleep, which came only when I resorted to my swag rolled out on the wooden floor.

The couple of days passed pleasantly, but, as always, there were a thousand-odd chores to be done. Cleo's pack sore was worse despite antibiotic treatment and had formed an abscess which had to be lanced and drained. We had at last obtained some fly repellant for these sores from the nearby town of Mt Isa. Cash had to be wired through from down south, travelling stock permits were required, supplies had to be reorganised and perished items discarded. But we had easy jobs, or so we were told later, for my mother and Rowan, my wife, had offered to do our washing, sadly underestimating the task they were taking on.

Most interesting for us were the local library and museum, where I spent absorbing hours poring over a Lands Department map of Western Queensland on which each of Burke's camps had been marked in. The author of this map was one Harry Towner, a local who, like myself, was an amateur in the field of history, but who had spent a lot of time searching through local records to locate marked trees which were thought to be on the explorer's track. He showed them well to the west of Cloncurry, and going north along the Corella and not the Cloncurry River, a proposition which seemed as feasible as some of the other historical maps in existence. In some areas it was obviously quite accurate—where, for example, he had shown them returning past the region of the three cones. In other spots he seemed to have them much too far west, showing them almost due south of 'the monument' when Wills recorded that it bore north-north-west on the compass. Still, he had put in a lot of hard work, and had produced what was the most accurate map to date. I felt a bond of friendship and admiration for this man whom I would never meet since he had died some years back, his work unrecognised.

There was time for more than research. At lunch, over a cold draught beer, a quick glance down the menu showed no dates or damper, no 'roo garni. Good! The choice then was either grilled local barramundi or rump steak. The barramundi, or 'barra', was fresh and in that state it is probably the most beautiful eating fish on earth while, unfortunately, that sold in the south is nearly always frozen and the sweetness destroyed.

It was a strange sensation to have the family there. I had changed physically and mentally as the trip progressed and at first they seemed like strangers to me, but this sensation quickly wore off and in what seemed no time at all they had to fly off and I had to get underway again, while we still had so much to say to each other. Their little plane rose up over the ranges to the south and grew smaller, a tiny bright speck lost in the shimmering heat haze. We returned to the reserve and the chores which had, until now, been put aside for more convivial pastimes.

Cleo's sore was improving but her temper was not and the four of us had a task to get her down and hold her there for treatment. Wallaper's stone sore was still tender so we decided to try on a set of camel shoes. We had been told how to do this by an old camel hand. Green bullock hide is soaked in water until it softens, then four ellipses are cut out, each one large enough for a camel's pad to stand in the centre with still sufficient margin to fold up over the foot and draw loosely together with a rawhide thong at the fetlock. The whole process is nowhere near as much fun as it sounds, particularly the part where you actually fit the shoe onto the camel's foot. The reserve was quickly hidden beneath a swirling cloud of dust from which ropes, men or bucking camels emerged only momentarily. At last Wallaper stood there booted and quite disgusted before taking his first tentative steps, high obstacle-clearing steps. Within a short time, however, he was walking normally and we hoped the problem was solved. Wills remarked at one stage that they 'delayed for the purpose of getting the camels' shoes on—a matter in which we were eminently unsuccessful'.

We allowed ourselves the little luxuries of tinned camp pie and tinned peaches before swagging down, with Wallaper still grumbling occasionally, in the cold night.

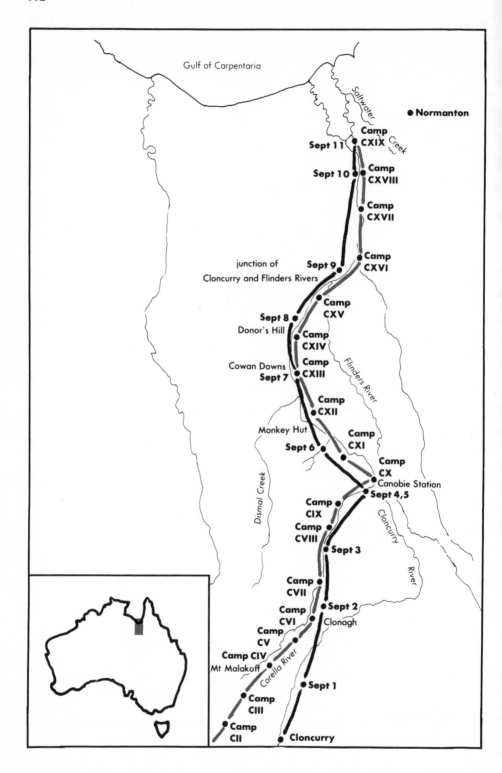

THE PLAINS OF PROMISE

We were underway early, heading north into the Gulf country. As we crossed a broad plain to the Cloncurry River I realised that today was my wife's birthday, but that was already another world away and here spinifex and anthills were looming up ahead. These occurred in patches of a half a mile at the most, this type of terrain being characterised here by the presence of blue peppermint gums. Initially the countryside was marked by rough, stony hillocks which appeared to be rich in iron or some other mineral, resembling the 'kopjes' of the Transvaal in South Africa, but later the country became flat, well-timbered and generally covered in Mitchell grass and Marshall grass, and the first thorny acacias appeared. These are a hardy shrub growing to nine feet or so, their succulent leaves well out of reach of stock and protected by long vicious thorns pointing up towards the tip of the branches. To our camels, however, they were the right height for browsing, and the thorns were no problem for them. They searched out the base of a branch, grasped it between tongue and hard palate and pulled the branch down, stripping both leaves and thorns from the stem.

We paused for lunch beneath a low ti-tree on the dry bed of the Cloncurry River, the luxuries of town not quite forgotten as we returned to our simple provisions without enthusiasm. The river bed was broad and sandy and scattered with smooth lucky-stones. The massive river gums on the banks carried flood litter high in their branches, serving as a reminder that the river is not always as we saw it.

At the first change after lunch we entered a thick eucalypt woodland with the odd, bright green Queensland bean tree appearing. As we made our way through the woodland, running parallel to the river, we saw the northern kookaburra for the first time, perched high on an ironbark preening his beautiful blue plumage. Unlike the kookaburras at home this species never laughs or, as one bushman put it, 'they only laugh when it snows in the Gulf'. The noisy lorrikeets made up for the kookaburra's silence, their shrieks ringing through the bush.

We camped not far from the river, and when we were unsaddling we noticed that Ginger had the hair rubbed off over one of his hips and had a nasty rash on the area where the padding had come away from the saddle and the exposed metal had rubbed. We treated him with Pharaoh's brew and let him wander off to join the others.

As we sat around the campfire we faced a dilemma—whether to follow the Cloncurry River as most historians suggested, or to cut north to the Corella River as suggested by Towner. The vague general description given of the river along which they had travelled matched our day's impression of the Cloncurry, so I decided that we may as well look at the Corella, too. In the six weeks since we left the 'Dig Tree' we had covered 778 miles and were not level with Burke's progress, but 200 miles remained between us and the shores of Carpentaria, and our allowed twelve weeks were half gone already. Even if we maintained this pace the rations on the return trip would be very thin, as Burke's were.

Dawn saw us already on the march, the countryside similar to that of the previous day. There were a few wary kangaroos on the flats, and an occasional wallaby, and here and there some fairly old bustard tracks. We had been talking around the campfire the previous night about crocodiles, trying to explain to Chilbi and Frankie just what a crocodile was. As crocs are found only in the far north they are unknown to the peoples of the central desert. 'Big uncle of Parentie' was as close as I could get. 'Lives all the time in big kwaja'. (A large animal related to goannas living in big waterholes.)

'How big this crocodile?' asked Frankie.

'Big as Wallaper and Larrikin together,' I said, exaggerating somewhat, and watched his eyes enlarge and whiten in the firelight, darting all around us searching the darkness for this monster which haunts the country ahead. Poor Frankie, he must have dreamt of crocs that night for he was up and off after the camels long before the sun was up.

In fact for some time now Frankie and Chilbi had been taking on more and more tasks of their own volition. It became obvious that somehow between us we had overcome a hurdle in our relationship. What I had initially regarded as laziness on their part was in fact reluctance to show initiative for fear of offending; unfortunately it seems that many Aboriginals have grown up with the knowledge that if a white man wants something done he will bawl out an order; until then it is best to sit quietly and wait. On his part the white man looks at the black man sitting there and concludes that he is just plain lazy. If we achieved nothing else on the trip it would have been worth it just to find out that this hurdle can be overcome by working together.

Without pausing for breakfast we set out north for the Corella River, marching along in the relatively cool morning air, passing in turn through gideah scrub, ghost gum woodland and grassy plains, the type of country which, in 1840, Captain Stokes had christened 'The Plains of Promise'. The day grew warm once the sun was up, and by midday we were walking through a steam bath.

His new shoes were obviously causing Wallaper great discomfort so we had to unload him and throw him over to examine his feet. The shoes had chafed the skin badly across the tops of his feet, and stones had found their way inside to bruise the pads. Paddy flung the shoes away in utter disgust, muttering under his breath as we resumed the march.

The painted roof of Clonagh hove into sight on the horizon, waving up and down in the oppressive haze, and we pulled in to refill the water-tanks. As we did so a horse in a nearby yard took one look at us and went berserk, racing around the yard and almost breaking through a railing fence in terror. A dozen or so other horses took not the slightest notice. The incident appeared not to worry the manager, Nick Murray, nor his wife, who treated us all to a sizeable working man's lunch. Unused to this ample fare during the day, both Paddy and I developed acute stomach pains as we rode that afternoon, and so, like a horse with colic, we had to force ourselves to walk and walk until the pain finally eased. We walked until sunset, then halted, throwing our swags down and falling upon them without further ado.

I had explained to Frankie that crocodiles only live in big waterholes and, since the nearby river bed was dry, he slept soundly and had to be shaken awake next morning. We saddled up and faced the 'gulf country' once again. The 'gulf country' is a crescent of black soil plains two hundred miles wide and stretching four hundred odd miles around the Gulf of Carpentaria, whose shores are lined with thick mangrove swamps. The plain is interrupted in places by low ranges, and is scarred by deep river beds which run only in 'the wet', carrying the run-off from the tropical downpours northwards to empty out into the shallow gulf. 'The wet' can start any time from November on and continues through to March, turning the plains into an almost impassable quagmire. Only essential maintenance is carried out during the wet, and those who stay on to do these chores have plenty of time on their hands to sweat, drink and sit listening to the rain. But in the cooler months, when the plains dry out and harden, the tempo of life quickens in time with the bellowing of the muster and the rumble of the road trains. While the people of the channel country seem as stoic and enduring as the dunes themselves, the men of the gulf country do everything, be it working, drinking or living, as if the wet may start tomorrow. They are a mixed and colourful lot: cattlemen and fishermen, prospectors and prawners, horse-breakers and croc-hunters, not to mention the strange flotsam of humanity which have been attracted to this lost corner. There is the hermit who lives in an old rainwater tank and another who tends his lawn carefully, having bordered it off with bleached croc skulls from the surrounding swamps. There was a charter pilot up there who, it is said, once captained international airlines until an unusual incident with two airline hostesses in a hotel in Los Angeles. On one prawn trawler is a deckhand who was once, under another name, a distinguished gynaecologist, while the skipper of another trawler can down a bottle of Scotch whisky without effect, but be moved to tears by a melody from his native Greece. The animals here are just as strange an assortment: deadly taipans and crocodiles, graceful brolgas and rare gold-shouldered parrots, agile wallabies and loose-skinned Brahman cattle, all of which contribute to the atmosphere.

When we reached the Corella River we were disappointed to find that it fitted Wills' description just as well as the Cloncurry did, and the positions given on the map are midway between the two rivers. We decided to follow the Corella from here on rather than turn back onto the Cloncurry since the two rivers would meet together in a few days anyway. By mid-morning we were bashing our way through a thick, thorny acacia scrub, when, out in the western sky, we saw a bright meteor in broad daylight, an event which seemed to worry Chilbi deeply, for he asked me many questions about it.

We descended the high steep bank of the river and followed along the river bed for a time, but decided it would be easier going and more direct back up on the plain. Getting up proved to be easier said than done, and the camels made hard work of the climb. But at last we made it, and all sat down to get our breaths back. We could readily understand the problem Burke and Wills were having not far downstream from here, when Wills wrote:

Wednesday, 30th January, 1861. Started at half past 7 am, after several unsuccessful attempts at getting Gotch out of the bed of the creek. It was determined to try bringing him down until we could find a place for him to get out at; but after going in this way two or three miles it was found necessary to leave him behind, as it was almost impossible to get him through some of the waterholes . . .

On the bank to our left I saw our first palm tree which coincided with the latitude given for Burke's 'Palm Tree Camp', but unfortunately these also occur at about the same latitude on the Cloncurry. Away from the river bank the thorny acacia grew thicker than ever, and we set camp early having reached a bore towards the northern edge of this scrub. As we came into the clearing around the bore we surprised a herd of wild pig coming in to water and Paddy shot two before the rest vanished back into the acacia again. By the time the first stars came out we had hams roasting over a good fire, our only worries being Wallaper's feet which were causing him trouble, and Cleo, whose pack abscess was not responding to treatment at all well.

The moon had barely risen when I got up and wandered the fifty yards or so through the acacia scrub to the bore and, as I was bending down to fill up the billy, I heard a sound which made me freeze. Somewhere, in the darkness behind me, something was moving, slowly and quietly towards me. I straightened up as carefully as I could and at the same time turned my head to try and spot the source of the noise, but I could make out little except vague shapes. All seemed quite still and I slowly relaxed, thinking that my ears had been playing tricks on me. Suddenly one of the dark shapes moved ever so slightly, one step forward, making only the slightest sound. Almost immediately another larger shape moved up two steps, and stopped. My fists tightened with fear as I had no idea what I was up against and, as I did so, the first figure moved forward again. In panic I swung at it with the only thing I had, a billy filled with water. The billy hit it and bounced off, clattering against the metal trough with a tremendous din. The creature gave a shrill squeal and bounded off, several other shapes, all around me, answered with similar cries and disappeared into the thorny scrub—bloody pigs! They had obviously come in to drink and hadn't seen me in the dark and the smell of fresh pig all over me had probably covered—or confused—my man smell. I laughed a nervous, relieved laugh as people do in such circumstances, refilled the billy and returned to the campfire to tell my story. Everyone roared with laughter at my fears; it was a story which would be told and embellished around many campfires at my expense. I think we are all a little afraid of the unknown.

Next morning, shortly after the start of the day's march, the river line broke up into numerous smaller tortuous channels and our path was frequently cut by small creeks, country in which it is impossible for camels to get into stride. Consulting the map we decided to head away from the river to a windmill which should soon have been visible on the horizon, and to follow a compass bearing of 31° from there, which should put us back on the river just west of its junction with the Cloncurry. That was the plan. We turned in the direction of the windmill and made our way across the wide Mitchell grass plain, mile after mile of waist-high grass, a hot wind blowing in our faces. Perhaps it was the grass rustling in the wind or some other unknown cause, but the camels became jumpy and finally bolted, galloping across the plain, ropes parting as each camel went its separate way before pulling up finally alongside a shallow line of bog-holes. We reassembled them and retrieved bits and pieces which had come adrift in the meantime. Hot and sweaty, we shared a swig from the water bottle and a curse on the mysterious nature of camels, then headed off once again. The windmill loomed up considerably to the right of where we had calculated but, thinking little of this, we headed for it, reaching it about midday. The ground for half a mile around it was chopped and pugged by the sharp hooves of cattle and boggy with urine and dung. It was also well populated with flies, so we moved off half a mile before squatting in a dry gully for lunch. A fence line stood nearby and I took a bearing along it, only to find nothing corresponding to it on the map. This started us rechecking and where the map had shown the windmill about four miles east of the river we had taken three hours to reach it. It dawned on us that the mill shown on the map twenty years ago was gone, the old fence line gone as well. We argued back and forth as we finished our dried dates (a half pound between four is surprisingly filling). Finally we agreed to head in the general direction of north by northeast until we caught sight of the river. We followed along the fence line for a mile or two before we became aware that the hot wind now blew stronger than before and the sky had become overcast.

'Big fire over there' Chilbi called. Far off in the direction from which the wind was blowing, great clouds of smoke rose hundreds of feet in the air. It was at least ten or fifteen miles away, but the wind blew in our direction and we estimated its speed at about ten miles an hour, blowing the fire across plains of long dry grass. We, on the other hand, could make only three or four miles an hour, and the river was not yet in sight. There was no need for panic as yet, but no time for smoko either. We moved faster, pushing the camels as fast as we could, our calf muscles aching and feet starting to blister with the unaccustomed lengthy strides. Our progress halted abruptly at a six-foot-high dog netting fence. There was no gate in sight and now was not the time to go and find one. Stripped to the waist we attacked it with a pair of pliers each, led the camels through and hastily restrained the wires and sewed the mesh back. We timed ourselves from whoa to go, sixteen minutes, or a delay of one mile at the present pace. Both Paddy and I had worked at fencing at some time in our pasts and I surveyed our handiwork with pride. 'Reckon that'll keep the dogs out for 'em?' I asked Paddy. 'Dogs, pigs, tourists, it'll keep the bloody lot out,' came the reply. It was another hard hour's travel before the river line came in sight on our left, but several fence lines stood between us and the river. We kept on our present bearing, pausing briefly at a waterhole surrounded by kurrajong trees. Slowly the tension eased as we realised the fire was not making enough headway to overtake us.

Late in the afternoon we stumbled out of the long grass onto a two-lane bitumen road, heading straight across to the river, only about four miles away now. We decided that although Burke and Wills probably did not follow this 'beef road', we certainly would in view of the fire which could overtake us if we camped the night this side of the river. Bitumen itself is very hard on camels' pads and soon wears them out, but the bore drain alongside the road, designed to take the run-off during the wet, was good going and it was along this we plodded, the pace slowing down now that our goal was in sight.

We climbed back briefly onto the beef road to avoid a stony gully, emerging onto the bitumen at the same time as a mud-splattered utility appeared from nowhere at terrifying speed, braking unevenly to a halt a few yards ahead of us. A beard appeared out of the window mostly hidden by a wide tattered hat. 'Shift those bloody yaks, yer bastard' it yelled by way of greeting, as the car door opened and a long angular body appeared below the beard. I approached, tired and cranky and quite ready to exchange pleasantries with this uncouth stranger or his cattle dog which barked support from the back of the utility. I had drawn close when he reached out, punched me on the shoulder and laughed. 'G'day you old bugger, you're still picking lousy bloody horses.' I recognised the voice this time as that of a close friend, a gulf country veterinarian known to his friends as 'the chopper'. He had heard rumours in one stock camp or another that we were headed this way and had driven down on the chance that our paths might cross long enough to boil a billy. He accompanied us across the creek, where we found a good camp site not far off the road. While we unloaded the camels and got the fire going, he shooed the dog off a pile of tarpaulin in the back of the ute, and from beneath the pile he produced a flourbag of fresh beef and a dozen hot cans of beer, 'Kimberley cold' he called them. We sat around the fire as the beef roasted, passing the billy and the yarns round while we waited. After the meal 'the chopper' rose and said he had better be going along as he was due to start TB testing a herd of cattle in the Territory, two hundred and fifty miles away, at dawn the next day. With a quiet 'be seein' yer mate' he disappeared into the darkness. As we sat around the last billy we discussed Cleo's pack sore and agreed to have a rest day the next day to give us time to lance and drain the wound and clean it out properly.

We crawled into our swags and for a while I lay awake watching the moon shining blood red through the haze of the distant bushfire, occasionally obscured by the ominous pall of black smoke. I dozed off, dreaming of bushfires all night.

A noisy group of apostle birds heralded in the dawn, the sun rising reddened and enlarged by the haze. We remained in our swags luxuriating in the thought of a rest day, no millionaire in a feather-quilted four-poster ever felt more comfortable. At last, driven by the need for a cuppa, I crawled reluctantly out, threw a bit of kindling onto the coals of last night's fire and wandered down to the creek to fill the billy. A shallow pool stagnated at the bottom of high mud banks. Curtains of thick green algae floated on the muddy liquid and the sleepy head of a tortoise appeared briefly through the slime. Although it was far from appealing the water would be all right once it was boiled. I filled the billy and headed back to camp. It was a tranquil setting, the thin column of smoke drifting up through the silver-grey leaves of the ironbark grove, three motionless figures relaxing on upturned saddles and gazing idly into the fire, totally at peace with life. The Australian bush may not appeal to everyone, it may seem drab when compared with the autumn colours of Vermont hillsides or the green of the Vienna woods, but it does offer the illusion of an endless peace. Once again the lassitude of the 'day off' set in, the drone of flies and the trill of cicadas blending with the murmurs of voices round the camp fire. But there was work to be done, and Frankie set off to track Cleo down, doing a slow wide circle of the camp until he cut her tracks which he followed west, finally disappearing into thick scrub. It was half an hour later before he reappeared with her in tow.

Meanwhile I had sterilised my instruments and had salvaged a little disinfectant and a few other items from the wreck of the medical bag. Paddy hushed Cleo down and roped her fore and aft, ready—more or less—for the operation.

In Frankie's absence two Land Cruisers had driven up and stopped opposite us, disgorging the TV crew who would be filming our progress to the gulf. It was good to see their familiar faces again and hear all the news, particularly the story of a beautiful girl following the 1700-mile gunbarrel 'highway' on her own with a couple of camels. Bob Connelly, the director, remarked that 'she had probably heard about you lot and was heading off in the opposite direction as fast as she could'. (I have since read her story and found this remark to be false.) While we listened to the news we treated Cleo: the abscess was lanced and drained, the dead tissue removed without incident. Cleo was a good and gentle patient.

By lunchtime our chores were finished, and we headed off for some barramundi fishing in one of the Land Cruisers. Calling in at Canobie, we were given directions to a good waterhole and instructions on the art of catching 'barra'. We bumped and rattled our way to the isolated fishing spot. Huge Papuan ghost gums shaded the thirty-feet-high banks which lined the river, a beautiful sweep of deep water on which pelicans and other waterfowl abounded. There were heads and backbones of huge 'barra' everywhere on the banks, but of live ones we saw nothing, not the smallest nibble. I remarked on arrival that a beautiful stretch of water like this was an ideal habitat for the freshwater crocodile, a remark which I think Frankie may have overheard, for he sat right at the top of the bank with his fishing line trailing limply down into the water.

After an hour of fruitless casting we decided to give it away and go for a swim. Clothes off, we plunged into the cold water and washed off the sweat of the trip and the smell of Cleo's abscess. As we splashed about Frankie let out a yell; he had a bite. We trod water while we watched him haul a small catfish ashore and, taking no chances with crocs, he hauled it slowly up the thirty-foot bank, his face wreathed in an enormous smile.

Later we returned the lures to Canobie Station where we learned that the fire from which we had fled two days earlier was now under control. We told them that their 'barra' lures were useless, at which they smiled politely and gave us about ten pounds of 'barra' fillets for tea. I think they were trying to tell us something, but in any event those fillets were the most beautiful humble pie I have ever had to eat.

The night was so hot that I slept on top of my swag wearing only shorts. Close by an owl called as I dozed off, lulled by Chilbi's snores. Sometime during the night I woke up freezing cold. Dark clouds hid the moon and a strong wind had come up, I crawled inside my swag pulling the canvas flap up over my head and slept once more, but briefly, for in what seemed only minutes later, Chilbi was gently shaking me awake, 'sun up boss, camels gone'. We searched for hours, with me exhibiting my tracking skills by finding their tracks which Chilbi, in front of me, had missed. I called him back to show him, a touch of pride in my voice. 'That track yesterday morning,' he remarked, and continued on up the creek. I followed somewhat crestfallen. We found Cleo and Frances a long way off and Paddy and Frankie found the others on the other side of the creek—they had crossed it early in the morning.

We saddled up and 'hit the road' again, heading up a rocky rise thick with sucker regrowth, wood swallows and apostle birds heaping scorn on our intrusion. This regrowth gave way to an open treeless plain after a few hours and here we paused for lunch beneath a solitary bean tree, trying to 'sing' a very wary Brahman cross heifer into our tucker bag for tea. 'Here bullock-bullock, here bullock-bullock.' We were out of luck again, so mounted up and headed off for a line of trees to the north. Abruptly the plain gave way to a blue peppermint forest growing out of a bed of red clay which was raised into numerous tombstones by termites. Between the tombstones grew spinifex and patches of scrawny native grasses. After some miles of this with a plague of locusts thrown in, we entered better country: tall eucalypts, bean trees and a scrub resembling mulga bush on the banks of Murdering Creek which crossed our path to empty out into the Cloncurry River. Here a large boar fell to our gun, and around mid-afternoon Paddy brought down an emu after which I rode with the severed legs of pig and emu slung across the saddle in front of me, flaccid toes and trotters tapping to the camel's rhythm.

We intended to camp that night at an old mustering camp shown on the map as 'Monkey Hut', meaning that we might have been camping indoors, a good thing as black clouds were gathering. We reached 'Monkey Hut' at nightfall, but the hut had an unpleasant smell about it, due to a dead dog under the verandah. We moved off and set camp alongside the nearby cattle yards. The television crew had left some time earlier, possibly a little put off by the prospect of sharing our emu and wild pig dinner. Dark clouds gathered as we ate, and spots of rain seemed to herald an approaching storm while in the gloom around us we could hear the rustling of pigs, the quiet night shattered occasionally by their squeals and squabbles.

As we made our way north along the river the thought struck me that while Wills had sketched the creek accurately on his map, he had given bearings, based on his star observations, which were some distance east of the creek, and in most cases the distance from the creek seemed about the same. Long after the expedition was over I returned to the Department of Crown Lands and Survey in Melbourne and checked the map in their vault. Each bearing given was six or seven miles east of the river. I discussed the matter with Rick Bailey, a navigator in the Navy, who contended that such a consistent error was probably due to a fault in the chronometer used to time star observations. A constant error of six miles to the east would most likely result from the clock's being twenty-four seconds fast, due either to the bumping it had received on the back of the camel or even to the temperature extremes they encountered. Intrigued by this, I checked all Wills' bearings back to the mountains and discovered something very interesting. Of the ten camps, eight are given bearings six miles east of the Corella River, one five miles east and one eight miles east. This would suggest that Burke had in fact followed the Corella, not the Cloncurry, and I noticed something else on the map to confirm this conclusion. Wills had sketched in mountains to the west of camp 104 and a larger mountain to the east. At the latitude he gives for this camp (20° 21'40" south) there are no mountains on the Cloncurry, but on the Corella stands Mt Malakoff to the east and more mountains to the west, just as he sketched them. Thus the question was finally resolved. But at the time we were still not sure, and cared little that night as we dozed in the light drizzle.

When Chilbi and I set out to retrieve the camels in the pre-dawn light we could make out the vague shapes of pigs retreating to their daytime haunts. While most of our wild pigs are certainly descended from domestic European pigs gone wild, it is widely held by hunters that there exists, in the gulf and on Cape York, a larger and more ferocious pig known as a 'Captain Cooker', so called because they are believed to descend from Asian pigs released when Cook's *Endeavour* went aground. These are said to be high at the withers and low at the rump, with enormous tusks and vile tempers, a type of 'super pig'. Cook's journal does record some pigs escaping and there are some very big pigs up here, but they don't seem to differ much in shape from pigs further south. They taste much the same, too.

The sun rose, penetrating the murky sky enough to reveal the camel tracks heading off towards a large patch of gidgee scrub where we found them kneeling down and ruminating quietly after their night's feeding.

We left 'Monkey Hut' with its guardian dog and soon found ourselves in thick brigalow scrub which extended for mile after mile, abruptly giving way to flat, open country around Wurung homestead. Here we called in for information about the ranges ahead and were given both advice and a welcome cup of tea before heading off again.

The going was good until Dismal Creek, black soil plains with fat cattle pausing to stare at us. On the other side of the creek the country became rougher, stony outcrops appearing and progress slowing accordingly. It was to be a bone-jarring twenty miles, with my back so sore that I could barely sit a camel for even a short spell. After a while, walking became a blessed relief. Emerging suddenly into a clearing we came upon a strange sight: a sward of forest half a mile wide had been flattened by some mighty force. The trees, some of which must have stood forty or fifty feet high, had been totally flattened, some uprooted and thrown yards away, all of them lying in the same direction. The ruin extended for a couple of miles, total destruction giving way to normal undisturbed forest again within a few paces. It was almost impossible to envisage any force which could confine so much damage to so discrete an area.

Descending from the high country with its unexplained mystery we struck the river flats, black soil covered in thorn bush thickets, ten feet high and seemingly endless, with cattle tracks and erosion gullies our only means through. Several miles of this saw us turn wearily back towards higher ground to the west where the sun was now sinking low in the horizon. At dusk, after much searching, we spotted the outbuildings of Cowan Downs, the station where we were to meet up again with the TV crew. The homestead is set on a barren hill of undulating red rock, a surrealistic lunar landscape made more so by dwarfed white gums which seemed to grow out of the solid rock. The homestead itself is a rambling two-storeyed building looking out over the plains. An atmosphere of old world charm and rustic comfort prevails there despite years of neglect.

Our hosts, the new owners David and Marcela, insisted that we all sleep inside 'in one of the dormitories' and since the clouds overhead looked ready to burst we readily accepted. Showered and scrubbed with teeth clean and fresh socks on we felt like new men as we sat down to eat. At that moment two stockmen appeared at the door, one holding his eye in obvious pain. He had been welding up a bore when a spark flew into his eye. I sat him under the kitchen light and rinsed the eye out, revealing a small gash on the cornea and a tiny metal chip beneath the eyelid. A torchlight search of our medical bag in the pouring rain produced one half-squashed tube of the appropriate ointment, enough to relieve pain until he could get to a doctor. Otherwise the night passed pleasantly, with lively talk around the big dinner table in an air of warm old-fashioned hospitality while the rain beat on the window panes and beds with clean sheets awaited us upstairs. We were not long in reaching them and were very difficult to dislodge next morning.

It was to be a fairly short haul today, with time off for the TV crew to set their cameras up and do some filming. About four miles north of the homestead we found ourselves on a wide lava flow devoid of growth except for a solitary species of tree which, like the dwarf eucalypt of the previous day, grows straight out of the rock. But these trees were totally unlike any I have ever seen, the trunk being smooth-barked and bloated like a bottle tree, supporting a handful of large green leaves and bright yellow flowers which exuded the strangest odour. The apple-sized fruit was not really appealing.

From here the country was obviously too broken for the TV vehicles to follow us and since we hadn't far to go we took three of the crew with us: Bob, the assistant producer; Ted, the cameraman; and Max, the sound recordist. The plan was for them to film and tape the trip from the top of camels, to give television viewers the feeling of riding a camel. It did not work. Not only did it not work, it was a disaster. In the first place the crew were unused to camels, but on top of that our saddle bags were full so that at the same time as they were concentrating on maintaining their seats they had to hold onto all the various pieces of equipment they had to carry, various pieces of which they shed like moulting ducks whenever a camel stumbled. Most of it Chilbi managed to retrieve, losing precious time backtracking to find a light meter or earphones, a film cassette or even, on one occasion, a stirrup. In the meantime, with one hand hanging onto the saddle and the other holding half a dozen different gadgets, they had no chance at all to ply their trade and it was a group of drawn faces which gathered round the waterbag for lunch. I had been a bit concerned that our provisions might not go round but I need not have worried; after a few hours on a camel they seemed to have lost their appetites. My first ride on a camel had produced a nauseous feeling similar to sea-sickness, and so I felt a little sorry for them now. We passed a fine waterhole surrounded by ti-trees, similar to one which Wills mentioned in his account of their return trip. Shortly afterwards, we pulled up for lunch alongside a shallow billabong which the pigs had turned into a stinking mud wallow, and the camels spread out to browse on the nearby thornbush. After lunch we each retrieved our camel, mounted up and headed off north along this pig wallow, and were a couple of hundred yards away in the time it took Max, the sound recordist, to load his earphones, tape recorder, microphone and tape cassettes onto Paddymelon and then mount up. Paddymelon, seeing his camel friends depart without him, bolted. From a kneeling start he hit flat gallop inside three strides. Max hung on grimly, a white face and clenched knuckles flashing through the scrub, with the sounds of Austrian oaths audible above the thunder of the galloping camel.

'He's trying to beat us to the gulf,' Paddy yelled as he headed off in pursuit. The race was to end almost as quickly as it had begun. Paddymelon, seeing a gum branch a few yards in front of him, simply lowered his head to clear it. Max had no way out and the branch caught him square across the midriff. For a second he remained there while the camel kept going, leaving him suspended in mid-air. The branch snapped abruptly under his weight and Max and all his gear crashed to the ground with the branch landing on top. The incident released the tension of a day of errors, and we laughed till we cried. Max did not join in with us, for in attempting to save his valuable equipment he had fallen heavily on his back and was in agony. We were about five miles from Donor's Hills Station, our rendezvous point with the rest of the TV team, and Max limped along valiantly beside us until the homestead came into sight on a hillside dead ahead. A cup of tea and fruitcake revived us before we left our passengers and headed off again. We had gone only a mile when the TV vehicles arrived with the news that some of the locals had organised a barbecue for us if we could possibly make it. It seemed a good idea.

We piled into the Land Cruisers and drove down the beef road to the 'Burke and Wills Roadhouse' run by the local veterinarian and his wife Judy. As is the lot of all country veterinarians he had been called away to treat an injured animal, but his wife and friends looked after us in grand gulf country fashion, plying us with prawns while gigantic steaks sizzled in their own juices. I was so preoccupied peeling my large gulf prawns that I nearly failed to notice Chilbi, staring horrified at his prawn covered plate. He leaned over and asked me in a whisper what they were. 'Prawns. Kurra marra, Chilbi. (Prawns. Good meat, old man)' I replied. He muttered in disgust and pushed the plate to one side. Frankie, translating, explained that Chilbi thought they looked like scorpions which he intensely disliked. Paddy and I had no such compunctions and helped him out. It was a feed to remember, and although it was very late when we returned to camp, we were glad to have made the trip.

It seemed only minutes later that the sun rose up over the river plain to the east and we were once again under way, rolling swags and loading camels. North of us the range rose higher into sandstone ridges and escarpments, so we crossed a broken, rocky knoll and headed out onto the plain to follow the river up. No entry was made in the diary during the original trip up through this region. But on the return journey they made a number of entries, just sufficient to enable us to pinpoint their whereabouts. On February 24, 1861, for example, Wills recorded their progress along the creek which 'creeps along at the foot of the ranges'. Sure enough, to our west, close on the river, stood Donor's Hills, not a great range to a cartographer and thus omitted from most maps, but a nasty range to a camel train. Pushing on, we lunched level with the junction of the Cloncurry and Flinders Rivers, the latter referred to by Wills as a 'branch creek with running water'. Ahead a spur of the Donor's Hills range loomed up, forcing the river to bend around to the east. An old Cobb and Co coach track went up over the spur, and to save a few miles we decided to take it. It was a steep climb and here and there the rut marks of the old coaches could still be seen, the stony path rising above the tall green timber to a level plateau from which the entire river plain below was visible, long green ribbons winding across a vast yellow landscape. The plateau was paved in red gravel, its surface so wide and even that a 'plane could land on it, but for a meagre growth of ti-tree, paper bark and spinifex. Our descent to the plains on the other side was rough going, the weight of the packs forcing the camels down so fast they had no chance to choose a safe footing and slid much of the way. The black soil plains, which had seemed so flat when viewed from the plateau, proved to be cracked by the heat into gilgais and broken up by the hooves of cattle. It was far from easy going. We crossed to a line of trees which marked a series of billabongs, and seeing one marked 'Paddy's Lagoon' we headed across to camp for the night, so that Paddy could see his lagoon. It was almost certainly the billabong along which Burke travelled by moonlight on February 23, returning from the gulf. We pitched camp near the muddy lagoon and boiled up some 'roo and parts of a pig, one of many which Paddy had shot that day. Cut into small cubes and added to a chicken soup it was beautiful. So was the swag, but tired as I was, sleep eluded me and I lay awake watching the smoke of the fire rise up to the stars above us. I had been lying there for half an hour and had just lit a last cigarette for the night when I became aware of something unusual in the southern sky, a flashing light moving from west to east at an incredible pace. After many nights of lying under the stars we had become familiar with satellites, planes and shooting stars, but this was unique, for it pulsated, bright then dim every second or so but moving much too fast for a 'plane. Finally it disappeared south of the Southern Cross. I searched the southern skies for a while, but as no little green men appeared I stubbed out my cigarette and fell asleep.

We had come over 900 miles in fifty days and had pulled away to a two-day lead over Burke, but the pace was telling, and the halfway point was still sixty-odd miles away. I slept poorly, my brain endlessly calculating rations and mileages, and wrestling with the problem of keeping the camels going at this pace for the return journey. The likely outcome of any attempt to return before spelling the poor beasts was becoming a recurring nightmare.

We were to be woken at dawn by a blood-chilling yell from Chilbi. As we had sat chewing our pig and 'roo the previous night the talk had centred on the nineteen-foot croc which had swallowed a man further north not long before. The attack had apparently taken place at a billabong not much bigger than the one on which we were camped. As I was telling the story I noticed a few anxious eyes searching the surface of the lagoon for anything that resembled a waiting crocodile, but only a couple of waterhens disturbed the stillness. I noticed that everyone (myself included) placed their swags so that the fire stood between us and the waterhole, and the fire was considerably larger than usual. Chilbi awoke at dawn after dreaming of crocs all night, and stretched out in relief only to feel something cold and scaly moving beside him under the blanket. His yell had us instantly awake, grabbing for pants, boots and rifles in that order. We slowly lifted the blanket to reveal a small tree goanna which had sought the warmth of the blanket. Relieved and feeling slightly ridiculous we uncocked the rifles and sat down to tell and re-tell the story, laughing more and more with each telling. We were laughing still as we saddled up and set out, but the laughter died down as we struck a black soil plain which had been chopped into a million potholes by the hooves of cattle in the wet. The rough surface was hidden by waist-high Mitchell and spear grass and we tripped and struggled slowly northward. It was impossible to ride, for the camels could not get into their smooth, swinging stride but jogged along stiff-legged instead, the shock being painfully transmitted through the rider's bottom to his lower back with each step. In addition, our path was crossed by numerous sharp erosion gullies forcing us to detour frequently.

Thus it was a great relief when a road crossed our path and for a while we could step out along it without dodging sinkholes. Our relief was short-lived for the road veered east and we reluctantly left it and headed northwards. Here the grass had been swept away in a recent bushfire and the sinkholes could now be seen rather than felt.

The tropic heat was intense and the air so heavy with moisture that our clothes were soon drenched with sweat, while perspiration from our feet collected in our boots to squelch as we walked. We took advantage of lunch break to empty our boots out, a rather foul odour greeting us as we did, overpowering the gamey smell of boiled 'roo tail. Boots on and bellies full we pushed on again, travelling across the plain parallel to the Flinders River.

The miles passed slowly as the sun edged across the western sky, the boredom of the plain relieved occasionally by a dingo track or some crows feeding on a dead pig. There were some trees off to the west but the heat haze all but obscured them and made it impossible to judge the distance to them. Finally, after travelling over thirty miles, we halted on the plain, lit a few sticks to boil the billy and lay down too exhausted to cook a meal. After half an hour Paddy recovered enough to dampen a handful of oats to eat and I tried chewing a stick of biltong but gave it away as being too much like hard work.

We lay back, drained, watching the gaunt shapes of the camels heading towards the setting sun in search of browse. They moved slowly now, ribs and hips plainly visible, a pack sore on Wallaper's right hip giving him an uneven appearance. With the Gulf of Carpentaria only a day's march away I found myself staring at bitter reality and sat sadly watching my theory go west with the limping camels. By tomorrow we would be half way, but already we had taken fifty-two of the eighty-four days Burke had allowed for the trip and there was no way camels in this condition could turn around tomorrow and make it back to Cooper's Creek in the thirty-two days remaining.

We had set out confident that we could do what Burke had failed to achieve, going from Cooper's Creek to the Gulf and back in twelve weeks, which meant averaging twenty-two miles a day, six days a week. We had maintained this speed for a thousand miles, but the effect on the camels was now clearly visible, even though they were carrying only half-loads. The humps, once well-filled stores of energy-rich fat reserves, were now all but absent, hip bones and ribs were covered only by skin, and more pack sores were inevitable. The stony plains and sandstone ranges had led to the pads of the feet becoming worn and bruised. Our camels were approaching a state of exhaustion which the Afghan cameleers called *zaharbahad* and their Australian counterparts called founder, described by an old camel hand, Major Glynn, in 1894, as 'a kind of dropsy, or poorness and thinness of the blood produced by overwork and absence of proper food'. Referring to camels carrying the heavy (400 lb) British Indian loads, he remarked that it is:

> ... better far to get 1000 miles out of him (i.e. the camel) in 80 to 100 days, in good condition at the finish, than 1000 miles in forty to fifty days, with a total and irrecoverable wreck, the probability being that you do not get through that distance. Overweighting and overpacing mean slow but certain death to the camel.

His words were echoed in 1917 by Dr Cross, camel specialist to the Punjab Government, who contended that for continuous work the pace should not be more than twelve or fourteen miles a day for poorly-fed pack camels and that an extra rate of only a quarter of a mile an hour makes all the difference, whether the camel will arrive fresh or fatigued at the end of the march.

On Greg's trip from Alice Springs to Gulgong, one thousand six hundred miles, he covered twenty miles a day with lightly-laden camels, but at each town he came to he spelled them for a week or so, thus their average distance per day was much reduced. It seemed then that it is the rate of walking which wears camels down more than the weight which they carry; it is not 'the final straw which breaks the camel's back', but an extra five miles covered each day. I was later to find out that this is indeed the case. Wilfred Thesiger, whose book I found only after the trip, was one of the very few Westerners ever to be fully accepted by the Bedouin tribesmen of Arabia; he lived with them for years, becoming fluent in their language and learning a great deal about their customs and lifestyle. After a time he managed to join up with El Rashid, 'the Wolves of the Desert', regarded as some of the most knowledgeable camel men on earth; desert raiders who will cover a hundred miles in a single ride.

In 1948 he accompanied them on an epic crossing of the 'dead quarter'. They covered the one thousand one hundred and forty-odd miles to Abu Dhabi at a slightly slower pace than ours (twenty miles a day), with their camels similarly loaded. (They considered the two hundred pounds-odd loads heavy as they prefer to travel light and fast , over shorter distances.) The El Rashid guides told Thesiger very early in the journey that carrying these loads at this pace the camels would without doubt develop saddle sores and possibly founder before they covered the distance. These 'uneducated' desert tribes must have understood the importance of loads and pace long before, probably centuries before, we set out.

I was later (oh, the knowledge of hindsight!) to come across a rare copy of A S Leese's book on camel medicine. He was a veterinarian whose expertise in camels came from years of experience with them in India, East Africa and Somalia, and he left no doubt at all of his thoughts on the matter when he wrote:

> An average distance for a day's march is 15 miles i.e. 6 hours for properly managed camels relying on grazing only and getting no rations. Under conditions of active service longer daily average distances can be done, but it is an abuse of the camel, and permanent transport cannot be kept efficient that way. A common fault with European officers with camels is to be in too much of a hurry . . .

In this last sentence Leese might well have been referring to Landells, Burke's 'camel expert', who covered the six hundred miles from Peshawar to Karachi at fifty miles a day with pack camels!

Of the various types of pack camel, some are bred for height and long limbs for long desert marches, while another type is shorter and more thickly built for mountain work. It was not recorded which type Landells purchased in Peshawar, but the paintings done of the expedition suggest that the finer desert breeds were used. Unfortunately, Burke's route was blocked by mountain ranges. He recorded the terrible suffering of the poor brutes, bred for the desert, as they crossed the ranges, 'the camels sweating profusely from fear'.

The facts of the matter lay clearly before me. Burke had set out to do twenty-two miles a day, but had not been able to maintain that rate. I had set out to show that, with light loads in the right season, it was possible, but I had shown the opposite. Had Burke maintained that pace he would have lost all his camels long before he was halfway back, as even with modern medical care, and the benefit of roads and tracks occasionally, our camels could not keep up the pace for much longer. Thus it was clear that the delay he would later strike with the wet season was not of paramount importance, as his camels would have knocked up in any season. The wet had, of course, compounded his problems, but his fate was already sealed.

It was a strange moment for me, sitting on the plain feeling that a year of preparation and a thousand miles of dust and sweat had done little else but prove me wrong. At this point, the feeling which had plagued my thoughts in recent weeks became a reality that had to be faced. This was the end for us. Across the burnt-out plain the sun finally set, and my spirits were lifted by the most extraordinary sunset I have ever witnessed, the sky glowing red, gold, green and blue in slow succession while two small pure white clouds floated across it. Gradually the blue turned to purple and steadily deepened until the first stars appeared. The peace and sheer beauty of it pushed aside all thoughts of defeat. I watched it for a long time in silence then fell asleep dreaming of camels well-fed and fit, sturdy great packers waiting in line at the Gulf, ready to haul us back to the 'Dig Tree'. But they disappeared in the light of dawn, replaced by our own faithful beasts who slowly knelt to receive their burdens yet again, roaring their disgust at life in general and us in particular.

We plodded across the plain, with Wallaper and Ginger pulling back, both leg-sore and weary. A bore loomed up in the distance and we made for it noting a mob of wild pigs around it as we drew closer. Paddy stalked them into nearby scrub, shooting one as they disappeared. Abruptly it turned and went for him, only a few feet separating them until his second shot dropped it in its tracks. It was a very near thing. Burke had mentioned to King that he hoped to shoot and live off pigs and buffalo up in these parts, but they had not reached this country in his time. We struck no buffalo on the trip, apparently very few stray so far east, but pigs were now commonplace and this one provided us with two good hams. We paused at the bore to water the camels and cut up the pig, then set off towards the river, lined now by thick forest and, closer in, by mangroves. On the far side of the river from us stood a series of low sandstone bluffs, 'Reaphook Range', originally discovered by the unfortunate Leichhardt who crossed the river here fifteen years before Burke. Wills had the journals of the earlier expeditions through this northern region, and knew the country ahead had already been explored. Indeed they had crossed the explorer Gregory's path the day before and thus Burke had already fulfilled his brief by finding a route to the known country in the north. Had they turned back here they would have saved a precious sixteen days, for the wet season was to set in and catch them on the black soil plains. But Burke had to be the first to cross the continent and there was no talk of turning back. King later told of their passing stony ridges south of their final camp, Camp 119. This must have been Reaphook, the only range hereabouts, so they were by this time on the other side of the river. We decided to cross and pushed through the thick forest, our progress held up by lianas, fallen logs and chest-high cane grass. At last we reached a narrow belt of mangroves, through which lay a pebble beach and beyond it a broad sweep of river, fifty yards wide. On the far shore a group of pelicans eyed us passively while nearby two green-black cormorants stood sunning themselves. We made our way down to the shore but when the camels began to sink into the mud we retreated, content to walk along the pebble flat in search of a crossing.

We noticed something on the beach and wandered over to find a four-foot-long saw-shark bill edged in sharp teeth, which fascinated Chilbi and Frankie no end. It took me quite a while to to explain to Frankie what a saw-shark is, and thus why we would not cross the river here. Having decided to make for the plain and cross lower down, we pushed back into the woodland which skirts the river. Passing a little south of a billabong I saw something floating in the water. We watched it for a little while, a partly submerged log which hung motionless, its yellow pupils taking in our every move. Not at all the frightening monster we had dreamed of, but a three-foot croc nonetheless. It would have been lucky to bring down one of the little agile wallabies. These seemed to inhabit the woodland in large numbers, but we saw no more of the nervous and pretty creatures once we left the timber and trudged back onto the plain. We finally crossed the creek by means of the concrete causeway on the Burketown road, and no more than a mile from the road we pulled up on the eastern bank of the river. Around us stood a circle of gnarled old box trees, some now dead, each one blazed a long time ago, the blazes in most cases almost overgrown. King told the court of enquiry that they had blazed some fifteen small box trees at Camp 119. We had reached their northernmost camp.

Wearily we unpacked the camels, noting as we did so that Wallaper's sores were worse than ever, and Ginger was starting to go the same way. The old man said nothing, just looked at the camels and nodded quietly. I could see it in his eyes, the timeless wisdom of the desert people who know what it means to go too far too fast in this country. Over a billy we talked back and forth, agreeing that the camels would have to spell for a couple of weeks to regain strength and let the pack sores heal before they could face that journey again. But two weeks were more than we could spare, time had run out and for us the trip was over.

RETREAT TO ETERNITY

The next day found us sitting at the bar of the Purple Pub in Normanton. John Barnes, the manager of Magowra station, was that day sending a truck across to Townsville to pick up some bulls, and had kindly offered to take our camels over in the empty truck. From there, after a spell, they were to be railed down to Gulgong, in the care of Paddy and 'John the Pom', a station cook we met on the way who wanted Paddy to teach him about camels.

Chilbi and Frankie were looking forward to their trip in the 'plane back home to Alice Springs, and I had my ticket to Brisbane on the next day's 'plane. Paddy, in his usual determined fashion, would gladly have waited a few more weeks for the camels to improve, then done the return leg of our trip living off the bush as best he could, just to complete what we set out to do.

In seven weeks we had covered roughly a thousand miles, only to find that my theory did not fit the facts. Although I was disappointed I could not help but feel that the venture had not been entirely worthless. We had seen some fascinating country and had all learned a lot from the experience, and now had a much better idea of the route Burke and Wills had taken and of the problems they had faced.

Physically we had come through well and, although I had lost about twenty-five pounds in weight, I still felt in good shape. Mentally we had overcome personal and cultural differences to weld together into a close-knit team. Had we the time and provisions we still felt we could have gone back to Cooper's Creek, but the camels could not return in the thirty-odd days remaining. Time had run out.

Out of interest, Paddy and I made the trip up to Saltwater Creek, a tidal stream fifteen-odd miles north of Camp 119. Burke and Wills had left the others, King and Grey, here to look after the camels, and had headed for the sea taking only Billy, the horse. But now the wet set in and the horse floundered along in the mud and rain until they hobbled it and continued to try to reach the Gulf on foot.

They were now in the land of the Yappar people, gentle fisherfolk who lived in two-storey thatched huts resembling giant beehives; people who had kindly guided the explorer Leichhardt across the river twenty years earlier. They were not changed much in 1861.

Here we passed three blacks who, as is universally their custom, pointed out to us unasked the best path down. This assisted us greatly ...

Despite their help Burke's hopes of reaching the sea were dashed as he found himself blocked by mangroves and flooded plains. He had to turn back. Standing there together in that lonely spot, Paddy and I could only sympathise with Burke and the enormity of the task which now faced him. As they waded back through the mud to Camp 119, Burke must have started to realise the predicament he was in. He had only twenty-seven days' provisions left and had taken fifty-seven days to reach the Gulf. One camel was already lost and the others were 'leg weary' and in need of rest, and on top of it all they were caught in the wet on the black soil plains. Had he known how things were back at the Cooper's Creek depot he would have felt even more worried.

After the earlier skirmishes with the Aboriginals Brahé could no longer take chances. Two men had to be on constant guard in the stockade, and while the third took the camels out to browse, the fourth man guarded the horses as they went further and further from the depot in search of grass. To make matters worse the camels were suffering from 'scab' and rats were now plaguing the camp in such numbers that up to forty a night were being killed. Brahé ventured out of the stockade occasionally and climbed a rocky knoll from which he searched the horizon for a sign of either party, but the desert was still and empty. The relief expedition was still three hundred miles south of the depot at Torowotto. The country here had had no rain since Burke passed through, and Wright's horses were starting to knock up. Several times the horses were left behind while the camels went on ahead until they found water. Their loads were then removed and replaced with water which they carried back to the horses, whose loads were then piled onto the camels to carry forward.

Progress had been slow with this coming and going across the scorched plain, and the few remaining pools of water were fast evaporating in the intense summer heat. On February 11, Wright remarked:

Every hollow was coated with dry sand, glistening and cracked ... The heat was excessive. The camels were unable to stand in one place more than a few minutes, lifting their feet from the hot sand in quick succession.

The suffering of the thirsty horses was obviously affecting Dr Beckler greatly when he wrote:

What a change had the want of the precious fluid effected in these animals! The glossy appearance of their skin was gone, their formerly round forms were pointed and shrunk, their eyes dull and motionless lay hollow in their cavities and, with their heads

lowered, they stood about the camp ... Each time they passed the camp they examined every bucket and every pot. From there they went over to the still glimmering coals of our fire where they hoped to find something to drink and, searching for pots, they plunged their noses into the mass of red hot coals.

It was grim irony that at the same time as Burke's party was beset by floods and tropical storms in the Gulf, his relief party was suffering the agonies of thirst in the heat of the centre. Far off to the west of Wright and his relief team, Stuart's South Australian team were also feeling the brunt of the sun; they were just north of the present-day Northern Territory border with South Australia and several days earlier Stuart's dog had dropped dead with heat stroke. In all, a bad time for exploration.

Burke had obviously been considering his position carefully, and on his return to camp he issued orders to halve the rations and prepare to start back towards Cooper's Creek the next morning, despite the continuing downpour.

They were to make only twenty-odd miles in the next four days, plodding knee-deep in mud down past Reaphook Range on the eastern bank of the river. Their provisions looked grim, only flour left now. To supplement this they started to pick and eat a spinach-like herb called portulaca which luckily prevented scurvy. It was to remain a great standby source of food for them all the way back as far as the Koolivoo region, and provide them with both vitamin A and C. So that threat at least was over. However, they had no meat nor could they spare the time to go chasing game as all hands were needed to push camels through mud. While Leichhardt had lived well in this country, eating wallabies, emus, ibis, waterhen and ducks (he caught forty-six in one day), as well as fruit and resins, Burke was forced to kill and butcher one of his camels, Boocha, during a break in the weather. To do this the animal is hushed down in the driest spot available and shot, its throat cut immediately afterwards and then the carcass skinned. All meat is cut away from the bone and then must be sliced into thin strips. This would be a long and tedious chore in a butcher shop, but one can only guess what it was like crouched knee-deep in mud without even a chopping block. The strips are then hung in trees to dry, where it is a full-time job keeping the flies and crows away, picking up the pieces which the wind blows away, and, at the slightest sign of rain, taking down the whole lot and putting it under cover. With the flies, the humidity and the intermittent showers, drying camel meat in 'the wet' would have been a ghastly task—'Plains of Promise' indeed!

But at least after two days they could now add 'ten sticks of meat a day' to their meagre ration as they set out again, moving down the eastern bank of the swollen river searching for a crossing. The first day's going must have been reasonable, prompting Wills to christen that camp 'Pleasant Camp; 5R'. In all likelihood they were finishing off the last of the fresh camel meat, the liver, kidneys, brains and tongue, parts which

124

cannot be dried. It was to be their last Pleasant Camp for a while.

Thursday, 21st February, 1861. Recovery camp; 6R. Between four and five o'clock a heavy thunderstorm broke over us, having given very little warning of its approach. There had been lightning and thunder towards south-east and south ever since noon yesterday. The rain was incessant and very heavy for an hour and a half, which made the ground so boggy that the animals could scarcely walk over it; we nevertheless started at ten minutes to 7 am and, after floundering along for half an hour, halted for breakfast. We then moved on again, but soon found that the travelling was too heavy for the camels, so camped for the remainder of the day ...

Friday, 22nd February, 1861—Camp 7R. A fearful thunderstorm in the evening, about 8 pm, from east-south-east and moving gradually round to south. The flashes of lightning were so vivid and incessant as to keep up a continual light for short intervals, overpowering the moonlight. Heavy rain and strong squalls continued for more than an hour, when the storm moved off west-north-west. The sky remained more or less overcast for the rest of the night, and the following morning was both sultry and oppressive, with the ground so boggy as to be almost impassable.

Saturday, 23rd February, 1861—Camp 8R. . . . The evening was most oppressively hot and sultry, so much so that the slightest exertion made one feel as if he were in a state of suffocation. The dampness of the atmosphere prevented any evaporation, and gave one a helpless feeling of lassitude that I have never before experienced to such an extent ...

Nonetheless, they forced themselves on and managed to cross the river, camping that night at Paddy's Lagoon. Here the weather cleared and they made their way down around the foot of the Donor's Hill Ranges, passing the 'ti-tree' spring near the spot where Max, one of our TV crew, had had his spectacular fall.

Although the weather had improved all was not well, for first Grey and then King began to complain of severe pains in the back and legs, and Grey of headaches also. From here they all began taking turns in riding the camels, but their condition was not to improve. The heat was so severe that they took to resting by day and travelling by moonlight, making their way slowly back, averaging only ten or eleven miles each night. On March 2, as they made their way south along the creek, they encountered Golap, the camel they had abandoned on the trip up, who now looked thin and miserable. He was able to keep up with the team for only a few days, and they then had to turn him loose as he was then so poor he was not worth butchering for meat.

But they soon had fresh meat anyway, in the form of an eight-foot python killed by 'Charley' Grey which they ate the following day. It was a culinary experience they were not to repeat in a hurry.

Tuesday, 5th March, 1861—Camp 17R. Started at 2 am on a south-

south-west course, but had soon to turn in on the creek, as Mr Burke felt very unwell, having been attacked by dysentry since eating the snake; he now felt giddy and unable to keep his seat. At 6 am, Mr Burke feeling better, we started again, following along the creek, in which there was considerably more water than when we passed down. We camped at 2.15 pm, at a part of the creek where the date trees were very numerous, and found the fruit nearly ripe and very much improved on what it was when we were here before.

They were obviously following their former route closely, mentioning 'former camps' several times in the next week as they made their way south along the river. Burke overcame the after-effects of his reptilian feast but Grey, who seemed to have also suffered from eating the snake, had hardly recovered when he again became ill. This time, Wills says, 'He caught cold last night through carelessness in covering himself'.

The weather had held off for the previous few weeks and by Sunday, March 10, they had recrossed the 'Plains of Promise' and once again faced the mountain country (and the Kalkadoons). They were still over six hundred miles from the depot on Cooper's Creek, and Burke's twelve weeks were already up. Back at the depot, Brahé was, as he said, 'Looking out anxiously for Burke's return'. For the four men, isolated on the creek, life seems to have been unutterably monotonous, each day as scorching and uneventful as the one before, the nights being scarcely any cooler and offering little relief. To break the monotony Brahé set out towards the east-south-east to search for any sign of Wright, but pulled up only about ten miles away from the creek. 'The country in that direction is very stony. From the top of the stony rise I saw a low range running E and W, distant about fifteen miles.'

No sign of Wright: Brahé now had to face the fact that something had gone seriously wrong down south, and that his own party (and possibly Burke's as well) might have to get back to Menindee on the provisions available at the depot. Burke would have none left by now as he had taken three months' provisions and his three months had elapsed. They had set out from Menindee with about six months' provisions, enough to last the eight men until mid-April. It was now mid-March and the trip back to Menindee would take a month. Thus, if Burke arrived back now and was fit to make the return trip, they would just make it. However, by killing whatever camels Burke brought back they would have another few weeks' grace. It all depended on Burke's early return and on the state of his camels.

But was Burke in fact aiming to return to the depot? Brahé was under the impression that he was not necessarily coming back that way at all, because of a chance remark Burke made on their farewell. 'If I am not back in three months, you may consider me perished.'

'Or on your way to Queensland', Brahé had suggested. 'Just so', Burke replied. Burke had also told McDonough, his friend from Galway, that he might be meeting a ship in the Gulf. There was still time, however, for Burke to show up, or, for that matter, for Wright to appear.

What had happened to Wright? He was at the moment in serious trouble, trying desperately to get his relief team across the now waterless plains south of the Bulloo swamp.

> **Monday, 18th February—Mud Plain Camp ... at 3 pm I returned to camp with Smith, having travelled at least 140 miles since my departure on the 16th. I found the country in front of the most fearful description. Mr Burke's track runs to the N.N.W., over some high ranges covered with sharp stones, and emerges upon the plains upon which we are camped, at a spot where it changes to an apparently limitless expanse of dried mud. The track is utterly effaced and the whole country the picture of desolation, not a vestige of herbage growing upon the plains ...**
>
> **Tuesday, 19th February—. . . Saddled and started with the horses at 7 am, the camels following half an hour later. A fierce glare, even at this early hour, rose from the plains, and the sun beat down overhead with an intense heat. Till one o'clock we traversed this weary plain of baked mud, skirting the sandhills on its western flank, and leaving Mr Burke's track, which ran more to the eastward. Not a sign of animal life was discernible, save the clouds of flies which tormented us throughout the journey.**
>
> **Friday, 22nd February—Rat Point. Rats visited us in myriads, not only gnawing through every pack bag, but absolutely biting the men when at rest. The horses suffering greatly from thirst ... During my absence I travelled upwards of 100 miles, crossing the country northwards in every direction without finding a drop of water.**

Wright was to set out again two days later in search of water. For two weeks he swept the country to the north for water, finding only a small drying-up swamp from which, he said, 'the camels drank greedily without any ill effects, but the men and myself suffered from it very considerably'. But he pushed on, he and his two companions now restricted to 'three spoonfuls of oatmeal per diem'.

On March 10, the day when Burke reached the ranges again, he returned to Rat Point, he and his companions suffering from dysentery. Of the five who had stayed behind to dig for water beneath the mud plain, he now found three showing signs of scurvy. Apart from the lack of water and the sick men, Wright had other problems. Burke's tracks were becoming harder and harder to find, and Wright lacked anyone who could navigate by compass or sextant 'white-man style', or, since his guide 'Dick' deserted, anyone who could navigate Aboriginal-style either. Without Dick, furthermore, he could not ask the local Aboriginals about the country ahead. I drove through this region a couple of times and to a stranger it is a terrible, inhospitable wasteland which dries out so quickly. It is easy, looking out over it, to see how even Sturt got trapped by it and to understand Wright's desperate situation.

Far to the north Burke's exploring party was following back down the creek which had led them to the Gulf and was now camped at the spot where it enters the ranges at 'the gap'.

Monday, 11th March, 1861—Camp 23R. Halted for breakfast at the specimen camp at 7.15 am, found more·water and feed there than before; then proceeded up the creek and got safely over the most dangerous part of our journey. Camped near the head of the gap in a flat, about two miles below our former camp at the gap.

Wednesday, 13th March, 1861—Camp 25R. Rain all day, so heavily that I was obliged to put my watch and field book in the pack to keep them dry. In the afternoon the rain increased, and all the creeks became flooded. We took shelter under some fallen rocks near which was some feed for the camels; but the latter was of no value, for we soon had to remove them up amongst the rocks, out of the way of the flood which, fortunately, did not rise high enough to drive us out of the cave; but we were obliged to shift our packs to the upper part . . .

Wednesday, 20th March, 1861—Camp 32R—Feasting Camp. We started at a quarter to six, but were continually pulled up by billabongs and branch creeks, and soon had to camp for the night. At the junction of the two creeks just above are the three cones, which are three remarkable small hills to the eastward.

They were unaware of it, but death now threatened in another form. S E Pearson was prospecting for copper in these mountains twenty-odd years after the event and later recalled how he ran across quite a number of elderly Kalkadoons who had been eyewitnesses to the passing of Burke's expedition through their country. They told him that, as the explorers were making their way south through the ranges, some of the young bloods of the tribe decided to attack them. To prepare themselves the warriors feasted on kangaroo meat and doubtless painted war stripes on their chests with the bright ochres for which the region is famous. It is doubtful if in their state Burke's party could have withstood an ambush, but his camels were to save him. There are three things in the lives of camels which they detest above all else: mountains, mud and hard work, and as the expedition made its way through the ranges in pouring rain the combination would have upset them considerably. Now when a camel is upset (as I know only too well) he lets out a roar like a constipated dragon. Even when one is used to camels it is a frightful noise, but the Kalkadoons were so terrified by these animals that they called off the ambush. For once Allah was on Burke's side. The exact return route through the mountains is uncertain, but on March 20 we can again pin-point their whereabouts.

They were back on the Burke River near Digby Peaks, and had probably slaughtered a camel within the last day or so, as they had a 'Feasting Camp' and also jettisoned sixty pounds of equipment. The party was now in the land of the Pitta-Pitta tribe, the plains of the channel country, and making their way south down the eastern bank of the Burke River. On the fifth day, an unfortunate incident occurred:

Monday, 25th March, 1861—Native Dog Camp—37R. Started at half past five, looking for a good place to halt for the day. This we found a short distance down the creek, and immediately discovered that it was close to Camp 89 of our upward journey. Had not expected that we were so much to the westward. After breakfast took some time—altitudes, and was about to go back to last camp for some things that had been left, when I found Grey behind a tree eating skilligolee. He explained that he was suffering from dysentery and had taken the flour without leave. Sent him to report himself to Mr Burke, and went on. He, having got King to tell Mr Burke for him, was called up, and received a good thrashing. There is no knowing to what extent he has been robbing us. Many things have been found to run unaccountably short . . .

King was later to refute part of this in court, saying that Grey received only 'several boxes on the ear with his (Burke's) open hand, and not "a sound thrashing", for stealing flour to make skilligolee or porridge'.

For the next five days they made a forced march down through the channel country, pausing only to get water and camel feed at the shrinking waterholes. Not only were the waterholes shrinking but the rations as well, the sharing of which King later described:

Mr Burke used to divide the rations; we had four plates and he put equal shares on each plate and covered the plates with his handkerchief or a towel and made us face from the plates, and then he requested us to call out a number—one, or two, or three, or four, so that no person could be favoured with a larger quantity than the others.

Somewhere near Koolivoo, that beautiful oasis, they halted.

March 29—Camels last feast; fine green feed at this camp; plenty of vines and young polygonums on the small billabongs.

March 30—Boocha's rest. Poor Boocha was killed; employed all day in cutting up and jerking him; the day turned out as favourable for us as we could have wished, and a considerable portion of the meat was completely jerked before sunset.

By now they had only three weary animals left, and were forced to jettison everything, clothes, blankets, instruments, the lot, to lighten the load because next day they had to face that desolate stretch where we encountered the strange wallaby. 'The neighbouring country chiefly composed of stony rises and sand ridges.'

The ordeal for those men of the forced march across this stretch of country must have been horrific but at last, on April 6, they reached the Diamantina, or 'Grey's Creek' as they called it. Greatly relieved they followed the creek south, finding water, shade and green grass in the riverbed. But the effects of the forced march were becoming evident.

Monday, April 8 . . . Halted fifteen minutes to send back for Grey,

who pretended he could not walk.

Wednesday, April 10—Remained at Camp 52R all day, to cut up and jerk the meat of the horse Billy, who was so reduced and knocked up for want of food that there appeared little chance of his reaching the other side of the desert; and as we were running short of food of every description ourselves, we thought it best to secure his flesh at once. We found it healthy and tender, but without the slightest trace of fat in any portion of the body.

Nearly twelve months later John McKinlay recorded how he came across this spot:

February 14th, 1862. Three miles north of our last camp passed the remains of Burke's horse and saddle, recognized them as his by camel dung being about the camp.

His position was about 26°20' south, 139°30' east, which means Burke's team was only one hundred and thirty miles north-west of the depot.

The four waiting men had long ceased to scan the horizons. Some Aboriginal families passed by on their way up the creek, and offered, along with presents of nets and fish, the news that a flood was due soon and that the whole area on which they stood would then lie under water. As Burke was now a month overdue and no relief had arrived from Menindee, there seemed no point in delaying much longer. Patten was slightly lame and one of his elbows was becoming very stiff, so he set about trying to shoe the horses before he got any worse, but the exertion proved too much, and in a short time he was bedridden. Brahé, himself suffering from pain in his legs and sore gums, and the two others, McDonough and Dost Mohammed, then had to complete the task.

It is a strange coincidence that at the time Burke was occupied cutting up his horse, one hundred and thirty miles north-west of the depot, Wright's relief expedition was now the same short distance away, but in the opposite direction, and it is evident that he was having just as difficult a time of it as the exploring party up north:

Sunday, 17th March . . . two of the camels, Goblin and Rangee, had very bad hump sores . . . one horse died from want of water and fatigue . . .

Monday, 18th March . . . one of the camels became very footsore and his load was distributed among the other camels . . . the whole of the camels were considerably fatigued by the heavy work they had lately performed . . . another horse died at Poria today from the effects of his push across the waterless plain . . .

As well, for some weeks now, three of the eight men had been ill, Ludwig Becker, the artist, and William Purcell, the cook, being so severely affected that they were left behind while Wright pushed on in search of water. Becker was a very cultured German, one of whose brothers was the tutor to Queen Victoria's sons, whilst Purcell was an illiterate, of whom Dr Beckler remarked 'his language is full of lower expressions than I have ever been compelled to listen to before'. Their life together in that camp was described by the doctor thus:

Two persons are left alone in desert country. There they are, a cloudless sky above them, an atmosphere without a breath of wind and totally devoid of moisture around them, on a shadowless desert receiving and refracting an almost intolerable heat from the early morn to the advanced hours of evening ... The heat and the glare of light around drive them quickly back under the roof of the tent ... They cannot converse with each other, because they cannot find one common subject of sufficient interest to both of them. Outside there is nothing to match the consuming heat but the unbroken silence.

... Sleep was impossible except as the effect of complete weariness, for soon after sunset when the numberless swarms of flies which had tormented them during the day began to disperse and to rest, the indisputable owners of these dreary grounds, 'the rats', made their appearance ... They would get a few hours' rest disturbed by numbers of rats which run and jump over them ... and which would wake them frequently by painful bites. Such was the life at Rat Point ...

It is to me one of the most heroic stories in the history of art, that while in these grim surroundings, and suffering the terminal agonies of scurvy and dysentery, Becker executed a series of beautiful paintings of which the detail and gentle style give no hint whatsoever of his predicament. It may seem callous to some that Wright had left them in this predicament, but he had little choice:

Wednesday, 3rd April—Koorliatto Creek. Seeing plainly that any attempt to move Mr Becker and Purcell would retard their prospect of ultimate recovery ... I resolved to push forward to Bulloo ... My anxiety to move arose from the fact that I feared Mr Burke's stores must require replenishment, and that any party left at Cooper's Creek would be anxiously expecting our arrival.

He reached Bulloo the next day, and found the natives here very hostile to his presence. Bulloo, however, was an ideal place to rest his sick men, a lake two hundred yards wide and five miles long, teeming with fish and waterfowl. He ordered his men to build a stockade, and set out north himself in search of Burke's tracks, which by now were five months old and almost obliterated. He had to abandon this search when Aboriginals lit fires around him to show their resentment at this intrusion on their last remaining waterhole.

On April 11, Burke's team set out for the final leg of their trip, on rations now consisting of dried horsemeat and water. Grey could no longer walk and so he was strapped to the back of one of the camels along with the dried meat. For the first few days they travelled over plains; stony patches interspersed with saltbush, claypans and the odd dry watercourse. The going was good, but Grey's condition was not. He was now talking of dying, and asked Wills to see that his belongings were sent on to his parents. While Grey was 'gammoning' (as they thought) Burke remained optimistic, expecting to see not only Brahé's and Wright's parties at the depot, but also a survey party from Melbourne.

Four days after leaving 'Grey's Creek' they were back in the sand dunes and now came the rain which the Aboriginals on Cooper's Creek had predicted, despite which the explorers pushed on across sandhill after sandhill through a torrential downpour which lasted, almost without interruption, all day. By four in the afternoon one of the camels, Landa, could go no further, so they halted on a small claypan between the dunes. The following day Grey's condition worsened and, after travelling only seven miles, he had 'an attack' from which time onward he was delirious. They pitched camp on a lignum swamp and covered him as best they could against the southerly wind, which blew so strong it kept blowing the fire out. In the morning he was dead, he had not been 'gammoning' after all. Perhaps a little guilty about their lack of sympathy, they spent the day burying him. They were so weak themselves that they found it difficult to dig a grave deep enough.

That should have remained forever as the end of Charlie Grey, a man who was once described by his former employer thus: 'A stout hearty man, and a better bushman would not be found.' But there is a puzzling sequel, for King stated that he had never noticed any scars on Grey, yet McKinlay, searching the region for Burke's party, wrote on Sunday, October 20, 1861, that he found a grave:

... rudely formed by the natives, evidently not one of themselves, sufficient pains not having been taken, and from other appearances set it down as the grave of a white, be he who he may ... removed the earth carefully, and close to the top of the ground found the body of a European ... two slight sabre cuts, one over left eye other on right temple inclining over right ear, more deep than left ...

Whatever the facts of the matter, Burke, Wills and King pushed on a couple of miles to camp on a nearby lake that night. They were completely exhausted and again the wind blew hard and cold—a forlorn camp it must have been. The next day they set out on their old course south-east and reached a branch of Cooper's Creek after a march of fifteen miles. It was dry and to shelter from the cold wind they camped on the cracked mud of the riverbed. Without swags or bedrolls they would have slept little in the frosty desert night, and got away early heading for the main creek. They reached it that afternoon, and were greeted by the Yantruwunta tribe, who had invited them to feast and dance on their outward journey. Incredibly, Burke again shunned their invitations, and instead marched on late into the night.

Friday, 19th April, 1861—Camped again without water on the sandy bed of the creek ... The night was very cold. A strong breeze was blowing from the south, which made the fire so irregular that, as on the two previous nights, it was impossible to keep up a fair temperature.

By the next night they were camped near the Queerbidie waterhole, only thirty miles away from the depot. By Wills' own account, they were in a pitiful state:

> **Our legs were almost paralysed, so that each of us found it a most trying task only to walk a few yards. Such a leg-bound feeling I never before experienced and hope I never shall again ... an indescribable sensation of pain and helplessness ... Poor Grey must have suffered very much when we thought him shamming.**

The camels were in only slightly better condition and any morning now they would hush down to take their passengers for the day's march, but be unable to get up. Lately they had managed fifteen miles a day, which put them two days' ride away from the depot. Burke made a bold decision that night; they would start at dawn, and keep going till they reached the depot. Tomorrow night they would feast on flour and sugar and tea and sleep in blankets under a tent, so the three let their hair down that night beside Queerbidie waterhole and ate as much horsemeat as they wished. In the dawn Burke mounted Landa and Wills and King climbed on board Rajah, the stronger of the two camels, and somehow both camels managed to get to their feet. They set off, sixteen hundred miles behind them and only thirty to go.

Wright had now no hope of being there to meet them:

> **17th April ... so many sick, and I thought myself still sufficiently strong to hold an entrenched position against any attack made by the natives.**

> **Thursday, 18th April—BULLOO—... stone rapidly got worse, being seized frequently with severe rheumatic pains.**

> **Sunday, 21st April—BULLOO—Throughout last night signal fires were burning around the camp here, and the natives imitated the howl of the native dog, apparently for the purpose of ascertaining our vigilance. Fifty-one rats were killed by means of a trap which I had made, but this slaughter, though greatly exceeding the subsequent nightly average, did not seem to diminish either their boldness or their numbers.**

Having only a pound or so of dry horsemeat left, Burke's team did not stop for breakfast or lunch but rode all through the day. As darkness came they paused only a few miles away from the camp to cook and eat the crows and hawks they had shot and when the moon rose they mounted up and rode off along the bank of the creek by moonlight. As they neared the depot Burke, slightly ahead of the others, called back 'I think I see their tents ahead'.

Finally, at 7.30 on the night of April 21, 1861, they pulled to a halt outside the stockade. Beside it stood a huge coolibah bearing an inscription:

DIG
3FT NW
21 APRIL, 1861

There was no one, the depot was abandoned.

EPILOGUE

When the day was over and the race was won,
No laurels awaited the man who won.
No thronging crowds to cheer and wave,
For the victor, nought but a lonely grave.

18th April, 1861—There is no probability of Burke returning this way. Patten is in a deplorable state . . . Being also sure that I and McDonough would not much longer escape scurvy, I, after most seriously considering all circumstances, made up my mind to start for the Darling on Sunday next the 21st.
21st April, 1861—Left the depot at 10 o'clock a.m., leaving 50 lbs of flour, 50 lbs of oatmeal, 50 lbs of sugar, and 30 lbs of rice buried near the stockade, at the foot of a large tree, and marked the word 'Dig' on the tree . . . We travelled very slowly, and halted at 5 o'clock p.m. having made about fourteen miles.

William Brahé

I flew back alone to Cooper's Creek, and stood once again beneath the 'Dig Tree', reflecting on the tragic events of the following few months.

Brahé's party, all now showing some signs of scurvy, were to meet up with Wright at Bulloo, only one hundred and fifty miles away to the east. The cavalcade turned south to Menindee, but were to leave four graves on the plains before they reached the outpost again. Burke decided that it was useless to try and catch them, his best chance was to follow Cooper's Creek west and then head south to a cattle property in South Australia, with the two camels to carry the stores which they dug up at the 'Dig Tree'. They buried their journals in the cache, with a note detailing their plans, and covered the cache up as they had found it, before slowly heading west.

They were stranded only twenty-odd miles away with both camels dead when Brahé and Wright rode up to the 'Dig Tree' for a final look. Seeing the cache apparently undisturbed, they finally gave Burke up for dead and returned to their own sick and dying. Downstream but a few miles lies Burke's grave, beneath a tall gum tree, and twenty miles away stands a cairn beside the sandspit where Wills died. Seven miles upstream from Wills' grave is the spot where, in September, 1861, an old Yantruwunter tribesman led Howitt to King, the sole survivor of the epic trip. In all, seven men died and many others suffered greatly. Dr Beckler later told the Enquiry that scurvy was the primary cause of all the deaths he saw.

It seemed strange to me that over a hundred years after Lind had established a cure for the disease, men should still be allowed to die of it. (By this yardstick it is stranger still that Scott's South Pole Expedition should lose men from scurvy in 1912.) When Burke's expedition set out from Melbourne they had taken with them sufficient dried vegetables to ward off the disease and had ascorbic acid to treat the disease should it occur. Yet it undoubtedly did occur, for Beckler's notes recorded exactly the appearance of the blue flabby gums, the numerous sores breaking out on the skin and the swollen painful joints in both Becker and Purcell, and in three of Brahé's party when they met. In struggling across the burning plain trying to keep the horses alive, no one had sufficient time to soak and boil the vegetables to make them edible, and scurvy was inevitable. Considerably weakened by scurvy, Ludwig Becker had succumbed to dysentery, probably contracted from the rats which had bitten him, as a typhoid-like organism (*Salmonella typhimurium*) has recently been isolated from kangaroos after contact with rodents in the same region. Burke, Grey, Wright, Smith and Belooch had all experienced 'dysentery' after eating native animals (possibly due to a similar organism), but none was affected for more than a few days.

While Dr Beckler had stated before the Commission that scurvy was the major factor in the deaths, his medical journal left room for serious doubt and in fact it was obvious that he himself was slightly puzzled. Herman Beckler was a graduate of Munich University, a medical school highly regarded in Europe, although his qualifications were not recognised in Victoria. But he was so highly respected by the medical profession in Victoria that he was taken on ward rounds by the chief surgeon at Melbourne Hospital 'because of his thorough knowledge of his profession'. In writing up the summary of the cases he examined on the expedition he remarked: 'All our cases of sickness were different from those cases of scurvy which came under my observation in this country and different from two cases I saw in Germany (cases of prisoners)'. He remarked that the usual skin sores and flabby gums in many cases were absent and that some symptoms he had not previously seen in scurvy were frequent, a swelling on the shin bone was an invariable sign, swollen knees and soreness and stiffness of the calf and thigh muscles, often with considerable swelling. The pulse rate was invariably high and a number of patients were anaemic and fainted frequently. But the one thing which struck him most was their utter weakness and inability to walk which he

The Discovery of John King

had not seen in previous cases of scurvy. He concluded: 'It was certain that there was a deficiency of some important element in the blood'. This was a very logical conclusion after treating apparent cases of scurvy with the known cure, Vitamin C, and still seeing the men die.

Dr Beckler, of course, was not able to cast any light on the deaths of Burke, Wills or Grey, but Wills was the son of a doctor and had himself at one stage studied medicine in London prior to taking up astronomy. Thus his notes, and the description of their symptoms, can be given some credence. King mentioned that both he and Grey were suffering pains in the back and legs, and that Grey finally grew so weak that he had to be strapped to a camel. Wills wrote, on the day they reached the 'Dig Tree', that their legs were almost paralysed and that the slightest effort induced an indescribable feeling of pain and helplessness. Many times in the next few months he was to remark on this weakness in the legs and arms in himself, Burke and King, and King recalls Burke's last steps, when he complained of the great pain in his back and legs. But of sore puffy gums, or skin spots, nothing was said; indeed they were eating native foods and vegetables heartily, and Wills was chewing Pitchery near the end, which would have been a painful process if he had had scurvy. In his last letter to his father he made the same astute observation as Dr Beckler had done.

Cooper's Creek
June 27th, 1861

My Dear Father,
These are probably the last lines you will ever get from me. We are on the point of starvation, not so much from absolute want of food, but from want of nutriment in what we can get . . .
Of portulac he said that 'the latter is an excellent vegetable and I believe secured our return to this place'.

He may well have been right, even half a pound a day each of portulac, boiling it as they did, would have provided them with an adequate amount of vitamins A and C. But their diet on the return trip of damper, camel meat and portulac would have been lacking in energy and would have provided only a quarter of the vitamin B_1, or thiamine, which they needed. On the trip up they had had plenty of thiamine from the pork.

Any zoo vet who has worked with seals and dolphins is familiar with 'Chastek's paralysis' caused by an acute deficiency of thiamine; stiffness in the muscles of the limbs and back, later paralysis and difficulty in breathing and finally paralysis, convulsions and death. Like scurvy, the disease is usually seen months after the relevant vitamin disappears from the diet. In the 1976 World Health Organisation Monograph on 'Nutrition in Preventive Medicine', two Japanese scientists documented the symptoms of beri-beri, the human disease caused by thiamine deficiency. In mild cases, they remark, there may be swelling only over the pretibial (shin) area, but even in these cases oedema (or watery swelling) is present in the calf muscle, causing intense pain. Other signs are wasting of the muscles, rapid pulse, anaemia, altered sensitivity to cold and increasing pain and weakness in the legs. Dr Beckler described all of these symptoms in his summary of this unusual outbreak of 'scurvy', and Wills' description of the suffering of Burke's team fits this picture much better than it does the symptoms of scurvy.

Brahé's team had run out of pork, their only source of thiamine, sometime in January, at about the same time as they used the last of the ascorbic acid. Towards the end of March the first signs of the dual vitamin deficiency had shown up.

Wright's men had been too busy on the upward trip to prepare their vegetables for eating and by March some of them had scurvy, which they had the means to treat. Although they had preserved pork and tinned mutton in their rations, they had conserved these for emergencies and eaten the salt beef, which contains only one-tenth as much thiamine as does pork. It is interesting to note that on the return leg, when both pork and vegetables were being utilised, the patients improved with the exception of one man, Dost Mahommed. He became steadily worse, his legs being almost totally paralysed by the time they returned to Menindee. He was a Muslim, a religion which forbids its followers to eat pork, the major, almost the only, source of thiamine they had. The reason that they had taken so little pork in the first instance was that Burke simply did not like it.

But the secret of the 'Dig Tree' does not end with Burke and Wills suffering from a simple dietary deficiency of thiamine. Recently some agricultural research scientists have by chance unveiled the last part of nature's grim joke on Robert O'Hara Burke. When investigating the cause of numerous sheep deaths in western districts, they found that nardoo (on which the explorers tried to stay alive) contains a poison which destroys the body's reserves of thiamine. In April and May when the explorers were eating it the plant is more toxic than at any other time of the year, and, because of the rain and the heavy grazing in the area by the depot party's horses, the plants eaten by Burke and Wills would have been particularly toxic new growth. That nardoo would obviously have been lethal to men suffering from beri-beri!

Beckler can hardly be criticised for failing to diagnose beri-beri since it was not recognised as a separate disease in Europe or Australia in 1861, being primarily a condition encountered in the Far East. (The name beri-beri, incidentally, is a very descriptive one for this dreadfully weakening and paralysing disease. It is Singhalese in origin and means, simply, 'I cannot, I cannot'.) It was not until 1882 that a means of preventing the disease was discovered by Admiral Takaki of Japan, who added more fresh meat and fish to the navy rice diet, and it was sixty years after the disastrous Burke and Wills expedition before thiamine was isolated.

If some earlier writers had taken the trouble to find Dr Beckler's journal (it is in the La Trobe Library filed under despatches, reports, et cetera) and to read of the horrors Wright's men were suffering, they might have regarded Wright's delays in a more understanding light than, for example, Frank Clune did when he wrote:

How then can we explain his conduct all through? Surely it must be, that he was a weak, lazy, undecided type of dawdler, who ought never to have been entrusted by Burke with such responsibility.

But Clune was merely echoing the sentiments of the Commissioners who, in 1862, reported to the Governor that 'Mr Wright has failed to give any satisfactory explanation of the causes of his delay, and to that delay are mainly attributable the whole of the disasters of the expedition, with the exception of the death of Grey'.

Can Burke be blamed for planning his trip to the Gulf at the rate of twenty-two miles a day rather than the fifteen miles a day which camels can maintain? This was the first camel expedition in Australia, and Landells, the 'camel expert', had boasted of his trip from Peshawár to Karachi with the camels at fifty miles a day. Burke cannot be blamed for heeding the words of the only camel 'expert' available, but rather should be commended for taking the word of this rogue with a grain of salt. With Ludwig Leichhardt, Burke will forever remain one of the enigmas of Australian exploration, for his errors were, on the one hand, his indecision and, on the other, his all-engulfing, single-minded determination.

Like St Peter, who thrice denied he knew Christ, Burke came undone when he said 'perhaps' on three occasions, for on an exercise of this magnitude there is no room for doubt. He told Wright that his appointment *may* be confirmed, or that another officer *may* arrive to lead the relief expedition, he told Wright and Brahé that he *may* send a team of pack camels back to Menindee to help bring up supplies, and he told Brahé that he just *might* meet a vessel in the Gulf or head for Queensland instead of returning to Cooper's Creek. No general tells his infantry commander that he may send cavalry to support the left flank, or that he just might direct his artillery fire in a certain direction. The seeds of doubt are deadly for they double the number of the contingencies.

But Burke's other error was in direct contrast to this: his stubborn determination to win the glory of the first crossing to the Gulf, to keep going when his supplies were half gone, and his readiness to starve rather than alter course, contributed equally to his downfall. Stuart, his more experienced opponent, turned back when he reached the limits of safety.

It seemed that the land, the failing camels and the deficient provisions had all conspired against Burke in his haste. Wills wrote, in his last letter, 'The great dryness and scarcity of game and our forced marching prevented us from supplying the deficiency from external sources to any great extent'. With these words Wills summed up clearly how their forced marching had put them out of step with the environment, an environment in which John McDouall Stuart acknowledged it was hard to explore.

Robert O'Hara Burke proved that to race across it was fatal.

ACKNOWLEDGMENTS

The expedition was made possible by the generous assistance of many individuals and organisations. The author is particularly indebted to the following for assistance in various fields:

The Australian Broadcasting Commission; The National Geographic Society of America; The Australian Veterinary Association; Beechams Chemical Laboratories; D G Hoskins (Finance); Professor Russel Ward and Professor 'Sandy' Yarwood of the History Department, University of New England; the staffs of the Mitchell and Fisher Libraries in Sydney, the La Trobe Library in Melbourne, and the National Library, Canberra (History); Mt Isa Mines; Doug Richards, Main Roads Department of New South Wales; Lt Col Mick Harris, 6 BTN RAR; Cmdr Don Chalmers, HMAS *Melbourne;* Howlett-Packard Co (Navigation and Mapping); the staff of the School of Food Technology, East Sydney Technology College; the staff of the Medical Faculty, University of Sydney; Roche Products (Provisioning and Nutrition); the National Photographics Index of Australian Birds (Photography); Professor John Keep, University of Sydney; Ted Finnie, Taronga Zoo; Dave Butcher, Western Plains Zoo (Veterinary Medicine); Dr Jan Hall; Traegar Transceivers, Adelaide; Royal Flying Doctor Service (Communications); Saliq Mohammed (Saddlery); D Cody, Taronga Zoo; Noel Fullerton, Alice Springs; Mike Steele, Innaminka; Cloncurry Shire Council and the people of western Queensland for their hospitality. Finally, I would like to thank my wife Rowan for her help and encouragement.